GOLD RUSH GHOSTS

*Strange and Unexplained Phenomena
in the Mother Lode*

by
Nancy Bradley
&
Vincent Gaddis

Photographs by Mike Kenoyer
Line Drawings by George Yesthal
Cover Design by Alien Heart, London

Garberville, California

International Standard Book Number 0-945685-06-8

Library of Congress Catalog Card Number: 90-60343

10   9   8   7   6   5   4   3   2   1

Published by:
Borderland Sciences Research Foundation, Inc.
P.O. Box 429, Garberville, CA 95440-0429 USA

Dedicated to:
William H. Bradley
My Dad,
My friend,
And the man who gave his kid
the guts to get going.
I love you,

N.B.

CONTENTS

"There are no unnatural or supernatural phenomena, only very large gaps in our knowledge of what is natural... We should strive to fill those gaps of ignorance."

Edgar D. Mitchell
Apollo 14 Astronaut

Preface

This is a book about ghosts, specifically apparitions that haunt the Mother Lode country. But what are ghosts? There is no simple answer for they represent a variety of conditions and situations.

The usual belief is that they are earthbound spirits bound to the environment they knew in physical life by habits, emotion or desire. They are lost souls, caught in the web of time. But there are other explanations.

Some appear to be thought-forms or spectral automatons, created by souls who have moved on into the realms beyond physical death. They may be formed by mental processes similar to those that induce schizophrenia or multiple personalities.

Then there are those who appear as visions from out of the "earth memory" or what are called the "akashic records" in oriental philosophy. The belief is that events that have occurred at any point on earth's surface are impressed upon the ethers surrounding our planet. Parapsychical literature is replete with accounts of such observations. A number of persons visiting the Palace of Versailles have seen the surrounding gardens as they existed in the time of Louis XVI and Marie Antoinette with buildings and paths long gone and gardeners working among the plants. And in England nearby residents occasionally see the Battle of Edge Hill reenacted with such details that the soldiers can be recognized.

Like a motion picture, the apparitions in these visions endlessly repeat over and over again some event that was emotionally charged. Other phantasms, however, seem to be portraying some aspect of the daily life that the spirit they represent experienced in physical life.

It is not surprising that ghosts dwell in the gold country. It was a time and place of violence and greed. Gold fever spread like the plague. Of the untold thousands, many died as the result of conflict and others lost their lives at the end of ropes. There were claim jumpers, gamblers and fornicators who drank rivers of hard liquor. Here the past equates with the present. You can feel it in the streets, in the old buildings that long ago housed saloons, gambling parlors, dance halls and brothels. You can feel this aura of timelessness in the very atmosphere.

Yes, there are ghosts in the gold rush country. Here are the stories of some of them.

1

SUTTER'S MILL
Where It All Began

The great discovery was made on a crisp January morning in Coloma, California. It was the 24th day of the month and the year was 1848 -- a day that would always be remembered in the history of the Golden State.

John A. Sutter and James W. Marshall were partners in the operation of a sawmill. Sutter needed lumber for his growing agricultural empire. He supplied the capital for the mill. Marshall, a skilled carpenter, superintended the building and operation.

On this fateful day Marshall walked over to the tailrace. The mill structure was nearly finished, but there was a problem with the waterwheel that would provide power. It would not turn properly. Water was backing up and the tailrace would have to be deepened. During the day some of the workmen removed boulders. At night water was allowed to flow and carry away the loose dirt.

Marshall looked down into the tailrace and noticed two tiny nuggets in the water. He scooped them up and hurried back to the building.

"Men," he said, "if I've found what I think I have, we're all going to be rich."

Sutter was skeptical. "Probably fool's gold," he suggested. "Iron pyrites look just like gold."

"What's the difference?" Marshall asked.

"Well, pyrites are brittle and gold is more soft. So let's make the usual tests."

The two men pounded the nuggets, heated them, boiled them in lye, and dropped them in acid. No doubt about it. They were gold! Marshall and Sutter laughed and shook hands.

"I suggest we keep quiet about this until the mill is finished," Sutter said. "I need that lumber." Marshall nodded his head in agreement. But the workers knew what had happened, and they were devoting all their spare time to looking for gold. Moreover they were finding it.

It was Sutter himself who broke the agreement. He told his friend

Sam Brannan, who operated a general store nearby, about the discovery. Brannan was an elder in the Mormon Church and several of the workmen at the mill had been members of the Mormon Battalion. Brannan hurried to the mill to collect the tithe from each Mormon. He trembled with excitement as he looked at the gold dust and nuggets.

Brannan had to go to San Francisco to change the gold into currency for forwarding to Mormon headquarters in Salt Lake City. When he reached the big city he lost all control of himself. He paraded the streets waving a quinine bottle containing the gold and shouting, "Gold, gold, gold from the American River."

Local newspapers confirmed the discovery. Within days almost every man in San Francisco had hurried to the gold fields. The fever spread to Santa Cruz, San Jose and Monterey. Homes and shops were abandoned, newspapers suspended publication, crops were left unharvested. What business remained was conducted by women.

Walter Colton, *alcalde* of Monterey, wrote, "The blacksmith dropped his hammer, the carpenter his plane, the mason his trowel, the farmer his sickle, the baker his loaf, and the tapster his bottle. All were off to the mines, some on horses, some on carts, and some on crutches, and one went in a litter."

Gold in California! The news spread like fire across a dry prairie. Then it leaped over the oceans: to the United Kingdom, to the European continent, Australia, and the Far East. And now the stage was set for the greatest mass migration since the medieval Crusades.

Seeking their fortunes, the people came. They came from the east in Conestogas and prairie schooners, wagon wheels turning, axles creaking, mile after mile across the Great Plains. They left behind them trails of broken wagon parts, bleached animal bones, and lonely graves marked by crude wooden crosses.

The magnitude of this migration is almost beyond belief. At one time westbound wagon trains passed between Missouri and Fort Laramie, Wyoming, in an unbroken stream for two months. One immigrant, James Abbey, is quoted in *California: A Guide to the Golden State* (American Guide Series) as writing that, "within fifteen miles he observed 362 abandoned wagons and the bleaching bones of 350 horses, 280 oxen, and 120 mules." For many on the western trek it was a time of sorrow and heartbreak.

Many came from the south. Overland some came over the old pioneer trail through the Anza-Borrego Desert, passing from the low to the high desert through Box Canyon. The walls of this narrow canyon had been widened by the Mormon Battalion to permit their wagons to pass. Later it would be used by the famed Butterfield Overland Stagecoaches traveling from Missouri to San Francisco and the Jackass Mail line between Phoenix and San Diego.

Continuing their journeys north from the southern desert, some migrants passed along settlements that were destined to become Greater Los Angeles, and up into the long San Joaquin Valley to reach Sacramento. Others followed the route of the missions, established a day's journey apart by Father Junipero Serra, closer to the coast.

And then there were the Argonauts. No, they were not seeking the Golden Fleece, but gold itself. According to the U.S. Census Bureau, by March, 1849, an estimated 17,000 persons had embarked for California from eastern ports for nine-month voyages around the Americas. Rounding Cape Horn, wooden ships and men of iron battled the fierce storms that came howling out of Antarctica. The small crowded vessels fought mountainous waves that swept the decks, scurvy and starvation. Not all of them made it.

San Francisco Bay became a forest of ship masts as crews and passengers abandoned their vessels and hurried to the gold fields. Chinese coolies, who had come to America as laborers, left their employers and joined one another in establishing prospecting camps. There they were frequently harassed by greedy and prejudiced anglos, physically assaulted and even murdered.

From the north came miners from Alaska and the vast provinces of Canada. While there were gold deposits up there, prospectors knew there were more opportunities to make prosperous strikes in California.

And so they came from the far places of earth, drawn like moths to the flames by the yellow beacon of wealth. Between 1847 and 1850 the population of California increased from 15,000 to 92,497. A decade later the U.S. Census enumerated 379,994 persons in the State.

Some came, not to look for gold, but to provide services or to prey on the miners. There were gamblers, skilled at double dealing, palming and bottom switching. While shuffling the cards, they could injog key cards and stack the deck right under the eyes of their fellow players. Others set up roulette tables, or sponsored keno, fan tan and other games of chance.

Then there were the camp followers, the dance hall girls, the prostitutes who came to service one of man's most basic needs and acquire riches in gold dust and nuggets. Disregarding the crooked gamblers, gambling and prostitution may be sins, but they are not crimes. Only in comparatively recent years have states and cities so designated them. The gold fields extended into northwestern Nevada. Ever since gold rush days, both gambling and prostitution have been legal in Nevada as is true today.

But even more popular were the saloons. Here, before any other activity, the miners could clear the dirt dust from their dry throats and feel the warm tide of alcohol as it penetrated their weary bodies. No cocktails, no highballs, no liqueurs here folks! Only raw bourbon whiskey. 100-proof, brought to the gold country in wagon trains from the corn states.

Operators of general stores became very wealthy, some making a thousand dollars a day. Prices were, as might be expected, high. An egg, for example, could cost five dollars. The miners, for the most part, lived on bacon and beans, eating enough rabbit food to keep from getting scurvy.

John Studebaker made wheelbarrows and sold them to the gold seekers. He returned to his Indiana home with his fortune and started a wagon manufacturing business. Toward the end of the century his descendants created what was probably the largest automobile firm of its day.

Originally the establishments devoted to necessity and pleasure were housed in tents. Amenities were nonexistent. An early historical writer, Hinton R. Helper, described one of the "best hotels." It was a canvas structure filled with dirt. Guests ate, drank and slept in tiered bunks in the undivided room. "When we creep into one of these nests," he wrote, "it is optional with us whether we unboot or uncoat ourselves; but it would be looked upon as an act of ill-breeding to go to bed with one's hat on."

Naturally in such an environment of lust and sudden wealth, it did not take long for crime to raise its many ugly heads. Adding to the domestic varieties of evil doers came the "Sydney Ducks." They were convicts who had escaped from the jails of Australia. Altogether, they turned San Francisco into the sin capital of the world. Fanning out into the gold country, they relieved the miners of their "pokes," then returned to the City by the Golden Gate to spend their loot in the saloons, gambling dens and brothels of the notorious Barbary Coast.

During the years from 1849 to 1856 more than a thousand murders were committed in San Francisco, with but a single execution. There was law but no order. To add to this sad situation, there was widespread corruption. There was practically no city government. In 1849 an alarmed official stated: "We are without a dollar in the public treasury. You have neither an office for your magistrate, nor any other public edifice. You are without a single police officer or watchman, and you have not the means of confining a prisoner for an hour."

In this hotbed of greed and conspiracy criminal leaders were in league with the politicians and bankers. One prominent man sought to end this unholy alliance. He was James King of William (who signed his name thus to distinguish himself from other James Kings), a very popular man among the city's decent citizens, who was editor and publisher of the *San Francisco Bulletin*.

The beginning of the end came during the summer of 1855. Charles Cora, an Italian gambler with powerful political supporters, shot and killed U.S. Marshall George W.H. Richardson. With thundering editorials in his newspaper, James King demanded the immediate trial and conviction of Cora. At the same time he bitterly attacked the adulterous marriage between crime and politics.

These editorials were assailed by James Casey, a rival editor and politician, who replied with some strong language of his own. His verbal assaults produced no results, so one day in May, 1856, Casey shot and killed King as he emerged from the office of the *Bulletin*. Casey surrendered to the authorities, confident of an early release. Just for the sake of appearances, they placed him in a cell.

The shock wave that passed through San Francisco can only be compared to the earthquake of 1906. At last the decent citizens had enough! Men gathered in ever-growing groups to express their anger over the cold-blooded murder of the well-liked King. The tolling of the fire bell brought the groups together to form a crowd in front of the police station. Casey's confederates slipped him out of the station and took him to the county jail. Here a large force of deputies and militia was assembled to protect him from the mob.

That afternoon and evening the citizens took action. A Vigilance Committee was organized. Under the leadership of William T. Coleman, by morning some 2,000 members had been enrolled and sworn to absolute secrecy. Thirty-three members were appointed to an executive committee. With morning more and more men, hearing the news, hurried to join the vigilantes until the total was almost 10,000. The executives' committee organized the men into military companies and equipped them with arms.

Headquarters were established in a mercantile building on Sacramento Street. It was fortified with a cannon and named "Fort Gunnybags." Now the vigilantes were well organized and ready for action. They marched to the jail, surrounded the building, and demanded Casey and Cora. The frightened authorities surrendered the pair without a struggle.

At Fort Gunnybags Casey and Cora were tried and found guilty. Lowered from the third floor windows so all could see, they died dancing at the end of ropes as the crowd of thousands cheered. The following day the large funeral procession for James King was directed down Sacramento Street past the now quiet, dangling bodies left there as a warning to other criminals. Later, after the priests had committed their souls to their maker, their remains were buried in the sacred soil of Mission Dolores.

As for the criminals, they had gotten the message. They scattered on the lam. We don't know where the Sydney Ducks and their ilk went as they fled for their lives, but they never came back to San Francisco. What followed was a cleansing of the worst aspects of the city and a reform of local government. Once the changes were in operation, the Vigilance Committee was disbanded.

But the city continued to enjoy its minor vices of gambling, heavy drinking and whoremongering. The Barbary coast continued to operate full blast until the earthquake of 1906. But San Francisco has always been a lively, tolerant, fun-loving city. And that's the way it is today.

Meanwhile, back in the gold fields, life had been continuing as usual with one exception. The crooked gamblers were fleecing the naive card players. Some of the gals in the brothels (not all) were picking the pockets of unsuspecting customers. The exception was that there had been a tremendous increase in the number of dangerous criminals who were robbing the miners and sometimes murdering them.

The leaders in the larger camps heard about the goings-on in San Francisco and they decided to take similar action. The word went out. Thereafter, any killer or thief who was caught had his neck stretched. At Placerville there were so many executions that the place became known as Hangtown. Here "Irish Dick" Crone, Bill Brown, and other notorious outlaws of the time reluctantly joined their ancestors.

Here, too, may have been the genesis of gallows humor. It was said that one condemned man with the noose around his neck remarked, "Folks, this is teaching me a lesson I won't forget." Another example is the doomed chap who halfway up the gallow steps paused and said, "Are you sure this thing is safe?"

Meanwhile, the miners continued their gold-seeking. In the earlier days they fanned out from tents and lean-tos. Then came the boisterous shanty-towns. They were given such names as Red Dog, You Bet, Angel's Camp, Git-Up-and-Git, Bogus Thunder, Shinbone Creek, and Lazy-Man's Canyon. In those days they could find nuggets on the surface. Sometimes gold was picked out of the rock "as fast as one can pick kernels out of a lot of well-cracked shell barks."

As the hordes grew, the nuggets disappeared and except for an occasional lucky strike or the discovery of a vein, the seekers turned to panning for the precious metal. On the average, it is estimated that most made about $50 a day at a time when a dollar was worth a dollar. Some made much more. From one panful of dirt $1,500 was washed. A trench 100 feet long yielded its two owners $17,000 in seven days.

Some of the miners managed to keep their fortunes. Most, however, "succumbed to the pleasures of the flesh and their appetites." It was the saloon owners, the gamblers, the brothel gals who ended up with the nuggets and bags of gold dust. Then, too, many a store owner took in $1,000 a day. Others who made fortunes for services were conveyors of water, innkeepers, owners of stage coaches and river steamers, and dealers in tools, pans and camping equipment.

What happened to James W. Marshall, who discovered the gold, and John A. Sutter, who proved that it was gold? It is ironic that the two men who inadvertently started the gold rush had their lives ruined by it. They ended their days in poverty and despair.

From the standpoint of material possessions, Sutter lost the most. When the historic stampede began, he had an agricultural empire. In 1839 Sutter, by swearing allegiance to the Mexican flag received a grant of 50,000 acres. In memory of his native Switzerland, he built a principality he named "New Helvetia." A fort of timber and adobe brick with twelve guns mounted on the ramparts was his castle. Here he ruled in baronial splendor.

On the land he built shops and forges operated by white workmen. Tractable Indians were his subjects. Trap lines were set for his fur trade. Herds of cattle roamed the pastures and foothills. And it was on his huge ranch that the town of Sacramento was laid out in 1848 and the first lots were sold in January, 1849.

Then came Sutter's Armageddon. Trampling immigrants and gold-hungry prospectors overran his land, stole his cattle, drove off his Indians, and challenged his rights to his property. His white workers took off to mines.

When he tried to get the squatters and miners to move, his life was threatened. There was no law enforcement agency to come to his rescue. In August, 1850, armed squatters rioted in Sacramento over the validity of Sutter's Mexican Grant.

In 1873 he gave up the struggle and moved to Pennsylvania with only a small pension for his services in the Mexican War. Seven years later he went to Washington, D.C., where he vainly asked Congress for the restoration of his property and an increase in his pension. Here in a cheap hotel room, alone with his memories, John A. Sutter died.

Shadows, too, marked the life of James W. Marshall. He attempted to claim a part of the Coloma Valley on the strength of his great discovery without success. The gold-seekers posted armed guards around their diggings to keep him out. When he appealed to the courts, friends of the trespassers sat as judge and jury; even his lawyers turned against him and joined the opposition.

Some prospectors considered his presence bad luck and ordered him to keep away. Others thought he had a supernatural gift for finding gold. They followed him wherever he went in hopes he would lead them to another rich strike. They went so far as to threaten him with death if he did not reveal the locations of gold deposits.

Poor management and bad debts finally ended the sawmill operation. Marshall turned to prospecting and occasional carpentry work. With his American-Mexican service pension he purchased fifteen acres for $15 and began growing grapes. For a time his agricultural project was successful. In the late 1860s, however, high taxes, increased competition, plus a decline in the demand for fruit, sent him prospecting again.

With the small amount of money he received from the sale of his vineyard, he joined two other miners in the operation of a quartz mine near Kelsey. When development of the mine proved expensive, his partners persuaded Marshall to go on a lecture tour to earn the needed funds. Pity poor James Marshall. To tell how he discovered gold in every detail required only about 15 minutes. A paid lecturer is expected to talk about an hour. How he managed to fill in the remaining 45 minutes is not known, but the lecture tour was a disaster.

When he returned to California, Marshall found that the glory days of prospecting were over. Twenty years had passed since his discovery. Large, well-financed business interests had taken over and consolidated all the richer veins of gold. Driving out the early miners and settlers, these powerful combines had the courts confirming their ownership of mines and lands.

In 1872 the State Legislature voted a pension of $200 a month for Marshall for two years. This was cut in half at the next session. Marshall used the money to equip a blacksmith shop in Kelsey. It, too, was a financial failure. The pension was renewed twice.

As so many unhappy, frustrated persons have done, he turned to the bottle for solace. Then in an effort to have his pension renewed, Marshall appeared in person during the 1878 session. When he raised his arm to emphasize a point, a bottle of brandy fell out of his pocket and skidded over the floor. Every eye in the chamber was focused on that bottle. His pension was not renewed.

The final years of Marshall's life were ones of sadness and privation. Occasionally he performed an odd job and he sold his autograph for pennies. He died in abject poverty on August 10, 1885 and was buried close to the spot where he made his discovery.

As mining camps became towns and cities, California remembered. January 24 was celebrated as Discovery Day. And the 18-acre Marshall Gold Discovery State Historic Park was created around Marshall's grave and the sawmill on the South Fork of the American River.

Over the years the original sawmill was vandalized, and what remained was washed away by floods in 1963. In 1968 a full-size replica of the mill was dedicated on Discovery Day. It is operated on many weekends and for tour groups, but the source of the power is not water but electricity.

The park contains many exhibits of the gold-rush era. There is a museum displaying placer pans, tools, stone-crushing devices and household articles. There is the Wah Lee store that served the Chinese colony, whose members patiently sifted sand and gravel after the earlier white miners had left. There is a typical miner's log cabin, gun smith and blacksmith shops, an ore car, two churches, the Robert Bell store, and the stone-walled jail with its iron door.

Marshall Monument
The final resting place of James Marshall. Unfortunately, he does not rest. His elusive shadow is seen stalking visitors to the site. His statue points in the direction of his gold find.

But overlooking all of the park's features is the bronze, larger-than-life statue of Marshall high atop a granite pedestal. One hand points down toward the spot where he made his great discovery. It was erected over his grave in 1890. Here in the park the visitor feels the weight of time and history.

Perhaps it is fitting, proper and not at all surprising that the first apparition in our survey of gold rush phantasms should be James Marshall himself. He was remembered and honored at last! Can it be that he has returned from the realm of shadows to enjoy the recognition and prestige that were denied him in his physical life?

Marshall not only believed in a hereafter, but he insisted he had spirit friends. He told his drinking companions that they would lead him to rich gold deposits.

When he felt the inspiration, he would start walking followed by frustrated but greedy fortune seekers who believed Marshall had supernormal powers. Unfortunately but invariably, the group ended up in locations that had already been worked over by earlier miners.

If the spirits had been right it would not have mattered. When Marshall staked out a claim, his pursuers staked claims around his. If there was any gold there, his followers got it.

Appropriately, the first manifestation of Marshall's psychic presence occurred on Discovery Day when the monument was dedicated in 1890. Witnesses said they could see the shadow of a man on the base of the pedestal although there was no object nearby that could have cast such a shadow. This is especially puzzling since the monument is on the crest of a small hill and somewhat isolated.

The elusive shadow has been seen at all times of the day and early evening, as well as different times of the month and year, making it impossible to chart a pattern for its appearances.

Typical of the reports of observation is that of the Harold Gomes family.

"I saw the shadow," states Jeane Gomes of Garden Valley, who along with her husband took their family to visit the monument in 1985. "I cannot believe that out of nowhere a shadow of a figure was before me on the marble statue and yet when I looked behind me, there was no one there to cast it." Harold also cannot explain the strange shadow. "It was only afterward that I heard about the strange legend. So, at the time of the incident, I could not find a reason for it, though I did try. I tried making hand gestures in front of me, thinking that the trees behind us were somehow through a quirk of nature casting the shadow. This was impossible however, as all shadows were facing in another direction. Then, the man's shadow moved to the side of the statue and down to the dirt and disappeared."

The shadow of the invisible man continues to be seen loitering around the imposing statue of bronze and granite. For centuries to come the image of Marshall will continue to point toward the location of his discovery. For it was this discovery that changed California from a land of Dons living on Spanish grants to the populous, widely diversified state that it is today.

2

COLOMA
Genesis of the Rush

It was in January of 1848, that the great world-shaking discovery of gold was made at Coloma. Thus to Coloma came the first waves of prospectors. By the following May an estimated 2,000 fortune hunters were in and around Coloma. By the year's end there were 20,000.

So that various aspects of our ghost stories will be better understood, some background information about that period in American history should be known. It was a time of passion, a time of avarice, a time of violence.

Tents were succeeded by hastily built structures. Several hundred buildings were erected with lumber cut at Sutter's sawmill. Some were hotels, but there was one saloon after another, interspersed with gambling halls and brothels.

The first gold had been found in the mill's tailrace, hadn't it! Moreover about two pints of the precious metal had been found on Mormon's Island, a nearby sandbar in the river. A group of frenzied miners reasoned that there was gold under the mill. They threatened to tear down the mill and end the settlement's lumber source. They changed their minds when some more sober-minded guards displayed their weapons.

"The whole of the region was in a ferment," writes Phyllis and Lou Zauner in their book *California Gold: Story of the Rush to Riches.* "An ant hill, just disturbed by some sudden alarm, affords apt illustration of the frenzy that invaded the entire population. Parties of miners flowed by in a continuous current. Everyone was afraid he should be too late, that he should not go to the richest places, that he should not find the fortune intended for him, that he shouldn't be able to return home the coming winter -- in short that he should not improve the present golden opportunity to the very utmost."

Very few of the miners, however, saved their "color." For gold, it was easy come -- easy go. Lots more out there. Let's enjoy our wealth for tomorrow is always a day ahead. We've had a rough day so let's have some fun tonight. In 1849 Coloma was described as a place of "strong whiskey, wild women, marked cards, loaded dice, and false weights."

Once at a bar a miner paying for his drink dropped a nugget. A man standing beside him picked it up and offered it to its owner. The miner looked at him in astonishment. "You must be a newcomer," he said. "Lots of that stuff around. Better keep that lump for a sample."

Days were marked by back breaking, wearisome labor as determined fortune hunters wrested the precious metal from the earth. At night hundreds of campfires crowned the Sierra foothills, throwing weird shadows around the camps. In the distance could be heard the pack cries of wolves and coyotes.

Strange stories were told around the campfires and in the saloons. Worse, most of them were quite likely true. A miner died. Other prospectors dug a grave and lowered his body into it. A preacher-turned-miner had just began his solemn eulogy when a mourner standing, hat in hand, at the edge of the grave glanced down at the departed.

"I see color," he shouted. Instantly the funeral came to an abrupt end. The body was quickly removed and everyone grabbed shovel and pick. The account does not tell us what happened to the corpse.

Another tale comes down to us from the past. One morning a woman in one of the camps awakened to find a baby in her bed. Seems she had given birth while she was asleep. We have heard of sound sleepers, but this comes close to being ridiculous. At any rate, let's hear three cheers for natural childbirth.

Hangings were festive occasions. When an impending execution was scheduled, the news spread quickly from camp to camp. The miners came into town by the thousands. To watch a fellow human meet his maker added a grim excitement to their work filled, drab lives. If they had a wife or girl friend in later years, it called for a picnic. And the condemned were expected to entertain the crowd before they were dropped into eternity.

Hangings were by no means uncommon, but in 1855 a celebrated double execution was conducted in Coloma. A brass band added to the spirit of revelry. The first prisoner was Jerry Crane, a school-teacher convicted of murdering one of his students, a girl named Susan Newnham. His only defense was that he killed the girl because he loved her. When it was brought out during the trial that he had a wife and several children back east, his goose was cooked.

Standing on the gallows, Crane sang some verses to the tune of a popular song of the day. He proudly announced that he had written the verses all by himself. It was evident, however, that had he lived he would never have become a great composer. "Here I come, Susan!" he shouted, as the noose was placed around his neck.

The second prisoner was Mickey Free, accused of being a member of a cutthroat gang that had been raiding and robbing Chinese camps and murdering isolated miners. While awaiting his execution, Free had written a confession, "Life of Mickey Free," that had been published by the local newspaper, the *Empire County Argus*, and copies were sold on the street. During his trial a member of the gang turned State's Evidence, and that fried his chicken.

While waiting for Crane to die, Free cocked his hat over one eye and tossed peanuts into his mouth. Once atop the gallows, he danced a lively Irish jig and was loudly applauded by the Irishmen among the spectators. Next he tried to sing, but his bravado faded, and he broke down completely. As the trap was sprung he was sobbing hysterically.

Coloma was once the seat of El Dorado County, which was established in 1850. Next to the building that served as the courthouse with its county offices was the Alhambra Saloon. Here the county officers quenched their thirst and played poker.

It was during a poker game one day that the county treasurer spread his hand and found he was holding four aces. He managed to retain a stony poker face, but ran short of money when the other players raised him. He sealed his hand and hurried next door to his office where he "borrowed" the county's assets of some thousands of dollars. He returned to the Alhambra where he wagered all of it. He was lucky. So were the citizens of El Dorado County. All he had to beat was three of a kind.

The residents of Placerville were furious when Coloma was chosen as the county seat. The bitterness steadily grew as arguments flew back and forth. In 1857 the tension reached a climax, and the Legislature ordered an election between Coloma and Placerville to decide the issue.

The election was probably the most outrageous in American history. In Coloma a merchant copied the passenger list from a ship docked in San Francisco and cast each name as a vote. In Placerville the polls were kept open far into the night so men from neighboring camps could ride in and cast their ballots after voting in their own precincts. The result was that the community had three times the number of votes as it had residents.

From Coloma stagecoaches made the rounds of adjacent camps. In both towns people were encouraged to vote as many times as they wished. When both towns challenged the results, the question was left to the Legislature which officially changed the county seat to Placerville in 1858.

The Chinese came to the Mother Lode country by the thousands. Naturally! They are world travelers. You will find them in the most remote corners of earth. If Robert Peary (or was it Frederick Cook?) had found a Chinese laundry at the North Pole catering to the Eskimos, we wouldn't have been too surprised!

To the gold country, however, they brought beliefs and customs that the other miners found strange and disturbing. They were brought to this country for cheap labor, the whites reasoned, not to search for gold. They were frugal with their money since many of them were sending it back home to their families in China. Unlike the high-living, fast-lane prospectors around them, few of them drank, gambled, or visited the cathouses. They kept to themselves, and were persecuted, discriminated against, and hated.

The Chinese came to Coloma. Here the worst racial incident occurred in 1861 after Henry Mahler sold the site of his former hotel to a company of Chinese. According to Mary Edith Crosley, in her book *Coloma*, "the Chinese began mining the land, which had also been claimed by a group of Irishmen as vacant mining property. The leader of the Irish was James O'Donnell. The courts ruled in favor of the Chinese, but the Irish vowed to dispossess them -- by force if necessary."

They met at the bar in Bell's store where they proceeded to get intoxicated. With alcoholic bravado, they marched noisily to the claim and drove the Chinese away.

"Let's go chink hunting and chase the yellow-bellies out of town for good," shouted O'Donnell.

They returned to the store where they added to their whiskey consumption. Then, author Crosley continues, "They headed down Main Street toward Chinatown, where they went on a rampage, wrecking and destroying everything they could lay their hands on. What they did not destroy, they stole. The frightened Chinese who managed to escape with their lives went into hiding. A few were killed outright and many were seized and badly beaten."

At this time Coloma had a town Constable. He tried to break up the mob, but they paid no attention to him. The officer had a pad and pencil and he wrote down the names of the rioters. The following day he made sixteen arrests. The rest of the trouble-makers went into hiding and some left the area for good. Coloma at this time also had a jail. The sixteen were convicted, placed in jail, and fined $200 each. Several spent nearly all summer in jail before their friends came forth with the money to pay their fines.

The industrious Chinese worked long hours and were satisfied to rework gold claims abandoned as worthless by other miners. Long after other miners had fanned out to other parts of the Mother Lode country, the Chinese were still finding color around Coloma. They were the last of the prospectors to leave.

The Japanese, too, came to Coloma. A federal census shows there to be 55 Japanese in all of the United State in 1870, and of this number 33 were in California. Twenty-two of these Japanese settlers were located in Gold Hill, the neighboring area southwest of Coloma. The first immigrants from Japan arrived in June of 1869 under the leadership of a noble

German soldier of fortune, John Henry Schnell, a follower of the Lord Aizu Wakamatsu. It is believed the colony started as a refuge for the ruling family, brought upon by the downfall of the Tokugawa Shogunate. They were forced to flee their motherland but brought with them tea plants, seeds, silk cocoons, bamboo roots, and as many other products of their native Japan as they could carry, in hopes of establishing themselves in the new land. It was arranged for Okei, a beautiful young Japanese girl, to come to America and serve as nursemaid for the Schnell family.

After a year of banding together, the colony knew it was in trouble. Poor soil, parched summer weather, and the changing direction of up-stream water by gold miners, as well as the failure of financial help to come as promised from their motherland, the colonists were forced to disband, many returning to Japan. Only two were to remain in the Coloma area, a gentleman by the name of Matsunosuke Sakuri and Okei, the young nursemaid. Both were able to secure employment with one of Coloma's pioneer families. Sakurai worked in the community until his death on February 25, 1901, after which his body was interred in the local Vineyard House Cemetery. This was accomplished without much ado, apparently putting his spirit to rest.

Okei was not as lucky. Legend tells us she hungered for her homeland. Often she would climb the knoll of a hill to be alone, looking off into the horizon in the direction of her birthplace -- Japan. She sickened soon after the disbandment of the colony, her body withered, and she died of fever, probably caused by her weakened condition. She was buried on her beloved knoll, to forever face the motherland she loved. Okei was forgotten until fifty-six years ago, when the gravesite was accidently rediscovered.

On a knoll, in the center of a cow pasture, is a lone tombstone, old and worn. It reads:

> In Memory of
> **OKEI**
> Died 1871
> Aged 18 years
> A Japanese Girl

Prior to World War II, groups of Japanese people visited the grave which they regarded as a historical monument. It is now on private property.

Dear Okei, in whatever realm you now sojourn after your short, event-filled life, we trust you have found contentment. We have no authentic reports that your restless spirit walks the earth.

They're all gone now. The miners, the saloon keepers, the gamblers, the ladies of pleasure, have all been dust for many years. Today Coloma lies dreamily on a curve of the slowly-flowing South Fork of the American River. The tiny town rolls up its imaginary sidewalks sometime around October 1 each year, and casually waits out another mild winter until the first of April when travelers begin flocking to this seasonal tourist town again. Coloma is mostly supported by the rafting trade and the vacationers, history buffs and occasional gold panner who comes to explore, examine and marvel at the place that changed the course of history. It is hard to believe that this sleepy, peaceful, out-of-the-way community of 900 residents, once inhabited masses of people in its town and surrounding hills. Today, minus the miners, Coloma is remarkably the same as it was in the 1800's, with many of the old buildings and historic sites of the gold-rush era remaining intact, as well as the legends and stories that accompany them. Eerie age-old bits of miners' skeletons, gold pans, and personal possessions are still found in the hills and streams, reminding us that the oft-greedy search for gold was a violent, turbulent one. It is no wonder that ghosts and spirits of these unfortunate people with dreams of gold, those that met bullets, hangman's ropes and pain in their last hours on earth, should still abound the hills, at the waterways, and old buildings of a long ago time. Coloma has been described as serene but spooky, even by the last remaining die-hards that "just don't believe in ghosts."

There are two store buildings in Gold Discovery State Park that are haunted, not by apparitions, but by sounds -- echoes from a long-vanished past. One is the Wah Lee (or Man Lee) store. It was built in 1858-59 by white settlers and leased to Wah Lee in 1860.

It seems Wah Lee had an astonishing repertoire of merchandise. According to accounts we have read, in addition to some banking on the side, Lee sold groceries, meats, prospecting supplies, hardware, clothing, furniture, and exotic Chinese teas, spices and dishes. Quite likely the wily Lee sold some other things we won't mention as this book is rated "G" and is dedicated to the survival of the American family.

Come with us into the Wah Lee store, now a museum. The interior is protected by a grill, but we have obtained special permission. We find seats. All is quiet inside the building. The only sounds we hear are birds singing in the locust trees outside.

Parapsychical phenomena cannot be turned on like an electrical switch. The psychic realm has its own laws that we don't fully understand. We must be patient. As we wait we think of the thousands of lives that these aged walls have known.

All should be still. But at night the park is dark, and sounds pervade the cracks and interstices of the old building. Unnatural sounding voices chill us frightfully. We have tapped into lives that have advanced into the unknown, leaving their spirits confused and haunting. Yes, we hear it, like waves breaking on a distant shore, it is the merged murmur of many voices faintly rising and falling in volume in response to some strange impulse. We look at each other, our eyes filled with wonder in the presence of the great unknown. We feel a chill pass through our bodies. The steady cadence continues and becomes louder. It is in Chinese and English, as the store served Caucasians as well. Now we distinctly hear the broken voices of an oriental man and woman, calling from long ago, humming the music of their motherland, as an invisible cleaver chops at a wooden block. Wah Lee? No one knows. But the sounds that come in the night are from someone, somewhere, from long ago...

The sounds begin to fade, slowly, back into mysterious time-space, the warp from whence it came. Then it is gone and the building is silent once more and we hear the birds singing in the trees. We step outside and feel we are walking from the world of the vastly deep to one of prosaic daily life. Our experience seems like a dream.

The clanging of a long-gone bell at Bell's General Store, also located in Coloma's Gold Discovery State Park on Highway 49, frightens visitors to the area as they recognize that they are stepping into ghost country. The brick building, worn to near collapse by the ravages of weather and time, was erected in 1849. One side of the building is a sorry, crumbled ruin, the rest is still standing, roofless, of its own volition, though it bewilders the imagination to understand how. Such are the remains of Bell's General Store.

But in 1850 it was a proud building with the distinction of being one of the only two brick buildings in the area. Bell, a clever businessman, knew that hungry, thirsty, dirt-encrusted miners would be in need of all kinds of commodities when they came to town. He intended to supply them with whatever supplies he could secure out of San Francisco, usually at unreasonable prices. Bell's was the only general store for miles around, so prospectors were in no position to barter. He smiled as he sold eggs for a dollar each, and whiskey to soothe a dry throat for ten dollars a bottle. Clothing, food, canvas, and gold-finding equipment were kept in plenteous supply. The store was used for other matters too. Many an important decision concerning the community and the lives of those who shared it was made over the bar at Bell's General Store.

As the need for this establishment erupted into the past, the hollow sounds of invisible merchandising could mysteriously still be heard within the structure. The clanking and clattering of canned goods, and shuffling of miners' boots continues on, even today.

And then there's the bell. How's that again? Yes, there's a spectral bell that haunts Bell's store. Presumedly honest, God-fearing folk insist they have heard it. Is the late Mr. Bell trying to ring up more business after all these years? Some speculate that Bell may have had a bell on the door to announce the entry of a customer. Any customers now would be wraiths since their physical bodies have returned to the earth.

We are told that the best time to listen to the sounds in both these stores is at night when the park is bathed in darkness. At such times this world that we are pleased to call reality comes closest to those other worlds that Mark Twain called the "greater realities." "This world," he wrote, "is but a reflection of the real realms that lie beyond our ken."

The other existing brick building stands a few feet away from Bell's store. It is the old Frank Bekeart Gunsmith shop, still a gunsmith shop operated by Bill and Libby Kelly of nearby Cool, California. They tell us they have had no supernatural experiences while in this building.

Too bad! What a shame! Ghosties, poltergeists, and "things that go bump in the night" add spice and wonder to our otherwise mundane lives.

Bell's General Store, Marshall Gold Discovery State Historical Park, Coloma, California. Do past customers' specters still linger?

3

COLOMA
The Spoor of Spooks

Contrary to some beliefs, apparitions are seldom associated with cemeteries. Ghosts may be earthbound entities, earth memory akashic images, animated astral body shells, spectral thought forms or whatever. Students of ghostly lore tell us, however, that they seldom display any interest in their decomposing physical bodies or their ashes in urns.

This includes, of course, the American folklore of "phantom hitch-hikers." Doubtless most of our readers have heard some version of this perennial yarn. A motorist picks up a hitchhiker of either gender. The hiker directs him to a certain spot which turns out to be the entrance to a cemetery. There the hiker vanishes.

The hiker has told the motorist where he or she used to live. Next morning the motorist goes to this home and is told that the night before was the anniversary of the hiker's death. Such tales can never be pinned down. It has always been told by a friend of a friend by another friend and so on *ad infinitum.* The intelligent reader (and all of you are) will quickly see there is no comparison between such wild stories and the cases we have collected for this book.

Ghosts are more likely to haunt the abodes they knew in physical life. These are usually dwellings, but sometimes they appear in hotels, pubs, office buildings, factories, on board ships, and in one widely published case in recent years, in the cockpits and galleys of airliners.

This latter reference is probably the most astonishing American haunting in recent years. In December, 1972, an Eastern Airlines Lockheed Tristar jet airliner crashed in the Everglades on its approach to the Miami, Florida, International Airport. One hundred persons were killed; there were no survivors.

Thereafter the apparition of Don Repo, the pilot of the doomed plane, appeared in the cockpits and galleys of Eastern Airliners for several months. His appearances were not warnings, but curiously were on crafts bearing parts salvaged from the wrecked airliner. An eerie rapport beyond our understanding. There were other psychic manifestations, one concerning the strange action of birds Don Repo had fed every morning he was home.

Witnesses were interviewed on the TV program "To Tell The Truth," and a number of TV and radio talk shows. For a detailed account see *The Ghost of Flight 401*, by John G. Fuller, Berkeley Books, 1976.

There are exceptions however. What would we writers do if there were not exceptions? One is here in Coloma.

A tall phantom woman taunts the tiny town of Coloma, as she keeps watch over an ancient broken tombstone in an old settlers' graveyard. Known only as the Lady in Burgundy, she beckons to motorists, visitors to the cemetery, and passersby, and then disappears, before ever getting her message known. The gravesite that she seems to watch so fervently, is occupied by three people, Charles Schieffer, who died May 27, 1864, at the age of 42 years. May Schieffer, died May 11, 1890, at 27 years of age, and tiny William Schieffer, who died March 28, 1861, at the age of 2 years, 28 days. Or so the marker says. They should rest easy, knowing they have their own special guardian. But no one here knows for certain, remembers who they were, or has an explanation as to why her spirit is still there. Should we presume that William and May were the children of Charles? But what about the mother? We can find no information on her. Therefore is it possible that the spectral woman represents the wife and mother standing guard over the physical remains of her family? Or does this spirit just happen to be in this location?

Since 1850, Coloma's Pioneer Cemetery, located across the street from the Vineyard House, has been the final resting place for early Mother Lode settlers. Also known as the Vineyard House Cemetery, buried side by side are 49er miners, pioneer farmers and their families, tradesmen, murderers and prostitutes. The two men executed from scaffolds temporarily erected in the front yard of the Vineyard House are interred here, as is Martin Allhoff, Louise Chalmer's first husband; Robert, her second husband, herself and their family. The plaque at the entrance to the cemetery reads: "Each contributed to California's colorful history. Please Respect Their Memory as you Visit."

Countryfolk wish the Lady in Burgundy would respect their privacy, as she disrupts the serene environment, and upsets the tourists who come to visit this historic town in the Mother Lode.

We do not know if she is, in spirit anyway, connected with the Charles Schieffer family. According to the Mother Lode Historic Society, all that is known of Charles, is that at his death he owned approximately $100 in personal property, and $800 cash. He was a resident of Coloma, and the year prior to his death, he paid $4.65 in state tax, $4.75 in county tax, and a poll tax of $2.00. This made him a respectable citizen. His occupation is lost in history, as is any further personal information.

The tormented entity's features are plain but strained. Her hair is parted in the middle and pulled back severely on both sides. She wears a modest-type shirt reminiscent of the 1800's, but her most remembered feature to those who have been startled by her apparition, is the long flowing skirt of deep burgundy.

An unusual aspect of this 'ghost' is that she is clearly seen in color. Many sightings from the past are displayed in black and white, or muted hues. Those who have witnessed the Lady in Burgundy remark of the color in her cheeks, if they are lucky enough to have seen her up close, or the blackness of her hair. All remark on the vivid color of her skirt. It switches as she turns and disappears before their very eyes. Day by day she stands in watch, beckoning with her hand to anyone who can see her to come closer -- to help. She appears ever protective of that plot in the cemetery.

"She seems angry, or concerned, and a bit frantic," stated Rosemary Dean, 35, a pretty, long-time resident of Coloma who has seen the ghost on several occasions. "Her piercing eyes look directly at you as she puts her arms out in a motion that says 'please come.' Then she turns to look longingly in the direction of the tombstone, and disappears.

"The first time I saw her I was walking past the cemetery in broad daylight," Dean continued. "It happened so fast that I took a double take to be certain it had not been the sun through the trees doing strange things to my eyes. But then I saw her again a few weeks later as I drove past the cemetery on my way to town. I was reluctant to tell my friends about her, but when I mustered the courage to do so, I was surprised that one of them had also seen her. Now it appears that she has made her presence known to many of the people around here. I wonder what she is trying to tell us?

"Still," Dean said, seriously, "I am hesitant to go past the graveyard when I am alone, and I will avoid doing so at night. I did that recently, and it was as if her spirit got into the car with me. My breathing became labored, and I felt a cold heaviness on my chest. She is a very strong personality, and I don't want to have that direct of a contact with her again, even though I wish there was something someone could do to help her."

Speculation runs high about who the Beckoning Specter in Burgundy is. Is she Charles Schieffer's wife and mother of May and William? Does she wish that people would help her find her family? Is she there simply to protect her loved ones from the curious that come and picnic, and sometimes trample the sacred remembrances of those long past? Does she have nothing whatsoever in common with the tombstone except that it is in the same location that she chooses to beckon from? It is on a hill, and she can easily disappear to the other side of the embankment from that spot. Why is she there? Who is she? What can we do?

In another section of the cemetery, on a modest slope is the grave of Catherine Schieffer, born 1862, and died 1916. Who is she? Is she involved in this mystery?

The Beckoning Specter in Burgundy

But who knows, as the mystery remains open to anyone to solve. We hope someone will, and we hope soon, as the Beckoning Specter in Burgundy has a self-imposed mission to fulfill, which apparently involves the help of the living before she can rest.

The Vineyard House

There is no doubt that the Vineyard House, Coloma's historic century-old hotel, is haunted. It is so proclaimed in literature distributed to tourists. Histories of the town where the Gold Rush began give us the details. The tragic story of this inn with a colorful past and a paranormal present has been told on such popular television programs as "It's Incredible" and "Bob Ripley's Believe It Or Not."

Today it is still a hotel with a restaurant noted widely for its fine food. The guests who dine here or rent a room, if they are fortunate, may witness one of the many appearances of apparitions. If so, they will have a fascinating topic for thrilling conversation the rest of their lives.

The Vineyard rests on a hill overlooking the town. It is a four-story structure, with nineteen rooms, nine fireplaces, encircled by a porch with a second-floor balcony. The style is Victorian, painted white with green trim. The interior contains a large ballroom.

It was built in 1878-79, erected to withstand the many years to come, sturdy and solid. As they say about automobiles and furniture, "they really knew how to build them in earlier times."

But the story of the Vineyard began years before there was an inn. It is the story of two men whose lives became strangely linked and who both experienced deplorable deaths. It is the story of Louise, the woman whom both loved. It is the story of the happiness and tragedies that interplay most of our lives.

Martin Allhoff, a German, and Robert Chalmers, a Scotsman, came to California during the rush of goldseekers hoping to make a lucky strike. They found some gold but acquired no great wealth. To supplement their findings they performed odd jobs until they had enough to travel back east.

They left for Ohio in 1852. We are not certain whether they traveled together or independently. Back in the Buckeye State Allhoff married a fourteen-year-old girl named Louise Wever and brought his bride across the country to Coloma. Chambers returned with his wife and two sons, Hugh and Abraham.

Disillusioned by the difficulties of gold mining, including the hard labor, competition, and the meager rewards, the two men decided to engage in other occupations. Allhoff became a vintner. He purchased some land that with later additions eventually totaled 160 acres. He lost no time in planting his vineyards and beginning his production of wines. The grapes were probably crushed at harvest time by the old world custom of dancing bare feet. The winery became one of the finest in the state.

Chalmers decided to become an innkeeper. He worked at various hotels until he had learned the business, then acquired the Sierra Nevada House. This was to be a unique hotel in all the gold country.

Meanwhile, Allhoff was living a good life and the years to come were bright with promise. He had a loving, dedicated wife and family. We can see him now looking with pride on his vineyards. Row after row of vines bearing Concord, Cataawha and Eden varieties of grapes glistening white and purple in the sunlight, acre after acre. Beyond were the wine cellars where their juices would be aged into multi-tasting delicacies. He was an excellent business man. Even now he was negotiating for additional properties. What more could a man desire?

And then the bomb fell.

Allhoff received word that his sales representative in Virginia City had been arrested for tax evasion. He hurried to the city, heart of the Comstock Lode in Nevada, only to be placed under arrest himself for alleged tax and license violations. He was ordered to remain in the city pending arraignment.

Mary Edity Crosley in her booklet, *COLOMA: California's Golden Beginning,* writes that the offense wasn't considered a serious one in this time of chaos in regulations and law enforcement. "He began to worry about being sent to prison and the shame and disgrace such an event would bring to his beloved family. Night and day he brooded until the idea became an obsession..."

Finally his depression reached bottom and he could stand it no longer. One morning as dawn was lighting the eastern sky, he retreated to an outhouse and committed suicide. His body was brought back to Coloma and buried within sight of his home and the vineyards he had loved so well.

Robert Chalmers was determined to be a real pillar of the community and a paragon of virtue. That is why, when he acquired the Sierra Nevada Hotel, he made a decision that was unique and surprising in the gold rush country. Guests at his inn would be limited to teetotalers. That's right, readers. We kid you not! It would be a haven for the sober seeking refugee from the thirsty barflies outside. All this in a region dotted with saloons and hotel bars like warts on a toad.

At first Chalmers waited in the lobby for his first customers, occasionally stroking his beard that was limited to his chin, with hope alight in his brown eyes. Once in a while a drunk who ignored the sign in front or was too pie-eyed to read it would stagger in the entrance. He was quickly propelled through the egress with stern words that, in effect, instructed him to get lost and to stay lost.

So he waited and waited and waited. Enlightenment came to him as he walked night after night through vacant rooms and glanced into his empty cash drawer. He was learning the lesson that the United States Government would learn years later. Prohibition will never be popular with the general American public.

Nevertheless, Chalmers did in time develop a clientele. For the most part they consisted of families seeking to protect their children from the influence of the dens of iniquity around them, of proselyting missionaries seeking to save the souls of the depraved inhabitants, and of sensitive mortals who were repelled by the noisy, rowdy and rough environment of the area. Then, too, there were civic affairs sponsored by Chalmers that brought lots of local people but little money to his establishment.

Looking for better financial worlds to conquer, Chalmers stepped out on the porch and cast his eyes like a fisherman with rod and reel over the community. His eyes came to rest on the vast Allhoff vineyards. Of course! Why hadn't he thought of it before? The widow Allhoff had inherited the vineyards, and winery and the cellars and all the other assets of her late husband. All she had to do was to see that the taxes were paid.

Moreover he had admired Louise Allhoff at a respectful distance. He could see her now in his memory -- her dark hair parted in the center, her gray eyes looking out quizzically at the world, her dignified, regal bearing. And he was twice a widower. Turning his back to the Sierra Nevada, he marched over to the Allhoff house to offer his services.

He was welcomed; it was good to have a man around the house again. Then, as time passed, the widow Allhoff became Mrs. Chalmers. The year was 1869, the beginning of a period of prosperity. Chalmers added more acreage to the vineyards and improved the winery until it became known as one of the finest in the state. Like Allhoff before him, his wines won prize after prize at the State Fair and special awards for excellence.

Allhoff had built two wine cellars in 1860 and 1866. Chambers added another in 1875 with a celebration attended by the Governor and other notables. All the cellars contained in a stone building are now owned by the state and preserved as a historical landmark. James W. Marshall came from his cabin home and placed signed personal papers in the cornerstone. Added to this time capsule were sample bottles of wine, newspapers and other articles.

In 1878, nine years after his marriage to Louise, Robert Chalmers began construction of the Vineyard House. It became the home for his family as well as the finest hotel in northern California. The grand opening was on April 4, 1879, with a large crowd participating in the festivities.

Then came the happy days. The Vineyard was the scene of all the social activities in the area. It was the meeting place of the elite, the *nouveaux riches* who had found wealth in the gold fields. Smiles were greeted with smiles. Waves of laughter echoed from the walls. Gaiety reigned. In the ballroom jeweled and perfumed ladies danced with men attired in their Sunday best. Around the bar geniality flowed with the drinks. It was perhaps the most enjoyable period in the Chalmers marriage.

A special guest during this time was ex-President Ulysses S. Grant, who answered questions about the Civil War and his administration. Chalmers used the occasion to announce that he had been elected to the State Legislature. He served one term.

Then came the sad years.

They did not begin with a bomb. No, it was a creeping, insidious menace as relentless as high tide along a sea shore. It began with Chalmers' loss of memory and Louise, of course, was the first to notice the beginning of her husband's decline. Next came the meaningless statements and acts. Finally came a short temper that threatened violence. Subconsciously, perhaps, he realized he was entering the realm of madness and he sought death. When a grave opened in the cemetery across the road, he would lie in it, his arms crossed over his chest in the traditional position.

Frightened for the children and herself, she had a cell with bars constructed in the basement. Here, in solitary confinement, Chalmers fell deeper into the mental darkness that engulfed him like a murky cloud. In the last year of his life came the final blow. He lost his eyesight. In this black, miserable world he moved helplessly and mumbled incoherently. No cell was needed now. Some member of the family or an acquaintance was always with him.

At last he accused his wife of trying to poison him. He refused all food and he literally starved. In 1881 death came as a friend and a savior.

Some writers have suggested that Chalmers suffered from the final stages of syphilis. Considering his conventional character and proud morality, this seems unlikely. Today a doctor might diagnose Chalmers' affliction as Alzheimer's disease. It is an extreme form of senility, sometimes premature, that attacks the central nervous system causing disorientation and then degeneration.

For a time all went well. Louise was an excellent manager and the Vineyard continued to be the scene of the town's social activities. Then came the greatest day in the hotel's history.

It was on Discovery Day in 1890. On this day the monument to the memory of James W. Marshall was dedicated. Marshall, who had died a lonely pauper five years earlier, was at last being honored with a lifesize bronze statue atop a high pedestal over his grave, his arm and finger pointing toward the spot where his discovery had forever changed California's destiny.

The governor and notables from throughout the state had gathered for the festive occasion. In anticipation of the event, a wing had been added to the Vineyard House. Two thousand guests were served ten-course dinners at the banquet under the direction of the efficient and gracious hostess, Louise Chalmers. All the community's residents and even some of the guests doubled as cooks, waitresses and waiters. It was a day to be remembered.

But trouble was brewing. Creditors appeared to harass the widow. A bank in Stockton announced it held a large loan on the property. A son from Chalmers' almost forgotten first marriage back in Ohio demanded his share of the estate and filed a civil suit. There were others with legitimate claims. It looked as if Louise and her children might lose everything. Her children included a daughter by Chalmers and two sons, Martin, Jr., and Joseph by Allhoff.

After three years of litigation, a judge deeded her the hotel and ten acres of land. Meanwhile the vineyards and winery were experiencing disaster. First some Chinese workmen she had employed fled in the face of racial discrimination. No longer guarded, the vines were ravaged by humans and animals. Next came a blight that killed the surviving plants and they withered away. The winery processing buildings fell into disrepair.

The bank foreclosed, but permitted Louise to remain on a rent paying basis. To meet her monthly payments she reduced room rents to keep them occupied and allowed the basement to become the town jail. Finally she signed over her remaining property rights to pay her attorney for representing her in the estate court cases.

When her lawyer died a short time later, his heirs sold the property to Martin Allhoff, Jr., and his partner. Thus a part of the property originally acquired by a father came to a son. Martin had his mother continue her operation of the Vineyard House, but he dismantled the other buildings with the exception of the wine cellars. The cellars were later sold to the state of California for permanent preservation. Louise died in 1900, a lonely woman with memories both pleasant and sad.

But strange occurrences had been happening. Robert Chalmers had died too soon after the opening of his beloved home and inn. Some part of his psyche, a spirit earthbound or perhaps an etheric double with biological memories, was determined to remain at the Vineyard House and enjoy his fondest creation. Tenants complained of mysterious sounds, of ghostly footsteps that echoed along the corridors in the quiet hours of darkness. One roomer fled in the middle of the night so frightened he refused to say what he had seen.

For many decades the Vineyard was operated as a run-down rooming house and restaurant under a succession of owners. During this time the weird phenomena continued. Guests, many of them who made hurried exits, reported they heard rustling skirts, metallic clangs and heavy breathing. It seems paranormal effects from one source can attract manifestations from other origins in a general psychic atmosphere.

Thus, a couple from Sacramento said they heard a group of noisy people enter the front door and start up the stairs. They opened their room door to quiet the revelers only to see three men in Victorian clothing vanish before their eyes.

The resurrection of the Vineyard began in 1975 when Gary Herrera, a former Oakland restauranteur, purchased the property in partnership with his brother and sister-in-law, Frank and Darlene Herrera, and a friend, David Van Buskirk.

They went to work on a hard labor of love. Floors, stairs and

The historic Vineyard House in Coloma. Now a restaurant and inn, it is haunted by a former owner, and many of his friends.

balustrades were stripped to the natural wood. Walls were papered. Paint was applied where needed. From dark corners of the attic came forgotten furniture to be refurbished.

"I thought I knew what I was getting into when I purchased the Vineyard House," said Gary Herrera. "I thought the house would be perfect for a restaurant and inn, and was anxious to put my plan into effect. There were many hours of hard work, reconstruction and modification before we could open for business. And, besides the years of neglect and age we had to fight to bring the building up to code, there seemed to be something beyond our control working against us."

No matter what plans Gary made for redecorating, it seems to be predestined. "I would painstakingly choose colors and fabrics, ordering vibrant shades for bedspreads, curtains, wallpaper, paint and accessories," Gary related. "My order would arrive in completely contrasting shades than what I had asked for. This was to happen consistently. Imagine my surprise when thumbing through an old Vineyard scrapbook. The colors and fabrics that had been delivered matched the original Vineyard House decor." Goose bumps climbed up Gary's arms. "I began to realize somebody from beyond our world wanted to keep this house the way it was.

"Actually, strange things began to happen right after I purchased the mansion," said Gary in retrospect. "A cup would be misplaced, a treasured bud vase would disappear and be rediscovered in some ungodly and most unlikely spot. We all joked about 'gremlins,' but inwardly we shrugged it off as absent-mindedness, because we were so busy. I chastised myself for being so careless. The more carefully I checked my every action, the more I realized it wasn't me. It was, and is, something beyond my world of understanding!"

"Same here," stated Frank Herrera, a man not given to believing in the supernatural. "My logical mind tried to come up with any understandable reason for the strange occurrences. I was reluctant to discuss with the others such things as curtains blowing when windows were closed, and cold drafts when I walked down otherwise warm corridors. Now I don't need an explanation for these things," Frank said, thoughtfully. "But it doesn't take those 'cold pockets' to give me the chills. I had shivers already."

David Van Buskirt was startled to find several old coffins under the porch during the restoration. It was known that several prisoners in the basement jail were executed in the front yard of the Vineyard House after hasty trials. Hasty burials followed and the coffins were probably kept available for possible future occupants.

Today Robert Chalmers' ghost bangs the walls when he is aggravated, and frightens the guests that do not meet with his approval. Most of all, his presence is felt in the basement, which now houses a downstairs dungeon-like pub, alongside the cell he once occupied. In life he was not a man sympathetic to the act of drinking alcohol. Chalmers' spirit seems especially critical of the activity surrounding the bar at the Vineyard House.

"One night while tending bar in our downstairs pub," Frank was to recall, "my customers and I were startled to see one cup in a series of eight hanging from nails on the wall begin to rattle for no apparent earthly reason. A hollow silence ensued, we were engrossed in watching the spectacle. The one cup banged and bumped against the others in random disorder. Then, the cup calmed, the clanging subsided, as suddenly as it began. I wanted to believe another freaky incident was over," Frank said.

Not so!

"A customer ready to resume his drinking, asked for a straight shot of whiskey to calm his nerves. I was happy to oblige," said Frank, "and perhaps have one myself! I picked up dual shot glasses from beneath the counter, and wrists up, placed them in tandem on the bar. I turned momentarily to grab the bottle whose liquid would fill the glasses. As I turned back, ready to pour, I saw the teetering and jumping of those two shot glasses, unaided by human hands, proceed to slide across the bar to the waiting customer. Empty!"

The customer's bloodshot eyes opened to enormous dilations, as he pulled his chair away from the bar. "He decided he didn't want another drink after all," said Frank slowly, thoughtfully, and non-flippantly. "If we have a ghost, he is a thoughtful one. The ghost figured the customer had enough to drink for one night. It was one of those rambunctious moods for our wayward spirit," he recalled. "And I was ready to close the bar for the night anyway!"

"I saw a ghost at the Vineyard house," stated a resident of the area. "My girlfriend and I had gone upstairs to look at the bedrooms which had recently been redecorated. To startle her, I turned the light out when she wasn't looking. There was a noise as if someone sat down on one of the beds, as you could hear the springs give. I thought it was my girlfriend and that my joke hadn't worked, so I turned the light back on. In front of us, sitting on the bed, was the figure of a man with a beard." His voice lowered. "The man stared sternly at us as if he didn't like the idea that we were in the bedroom. All of a sudden he began to fade, and we ran down the stairs." The man thought about the situation. "My guess is that it was Robert Chalmers that we saw. There is a picture hanging on the wall in the living room of the Vineyard House, and the spirit sure looked like his face. And it was his bedroom that we were in!"

Other guests to the Vineyard House have heard the calling of wild birds in the hallway between the upstairs bedrooms. Overnight guests have sometimes complained of someone trying to turn their locked doorknobs after they have retired for the night, or to awaken in the morning with their bedroom door being open.

"I was a housekeeper for the Vineyard House," a former employee said. "One day while I was alone in the house, the phone rang while I was working in the bedroom. I went downstairs to answer it. When I returned to the bedroom, there was an indentation on the bed that I had just made, indicating that someone had laid down on the bedspread. The indentation was a definite outline of a reclining body." She smiled a knowing smile. "Someone had laid on the newly made bed. I got the heck out of there and don't ever expect to return!"

On the other hand, some people are 'dying' to get hired on. "Think of the adventure in it," one hopeful said. Other employees at the Vineyard House get used to ghostly pranks. "I was once locked in the Vineyard House ladies' restroom for over an hour," one employee told us. "I had to wait until someone came along to unlock the door from the outside."

The community seems to accept the Vineyard House as being haunted. There are a few that wouldn't set foot in the place if you paid them, but the majority of the customers enjoy the spooky atmosphere along with the good food and accommodations.

But we suggest you see for yourself. True ghost watchers should not miss the Vineyard House, a real 'haunting' experience.

Today the inn is a fascinating combination of the heritage of a colorful past with the advantages of modernity. In the dining room a fire burns in a Franklin stove. The tables display brown-and-white checkered cloths centered with kerosene-burning lamps. Some of the chinaware came with the house. Other dishes and silverware were contributed by older Coloma residents. Patterns therefore vary.

The food is old-fashioned homemade country cookery. There are large bowls of salad and pots of soup and you serve yourself. The bread is freshly baked.

Each of the bedrooms are different. Each room is named after a famous person from the Gold Rush era, such as the Lola Montez suite, and the Lottie Crabtree bedroom. Some have brass bedsteads, others have huge Victorian foot and headboards. The community bathroom is floored with simulated brick and the walls are attractively papered.

Perhaps Robert Chalmers already knows how his Vineyard House has been reborn as he roams proudly about his creation. And Louise, wherever she is, if she knows, must be happy.

4

PROSPECTOR ROAD
Some Haunted Highways

There are roads that cross the vast expanse of deserts, that wind through mountains, that pass through shaded forests. There are roads that follow ancient Indian trails, that lead to yesteryears past abandoned farmhouses and sagging barns where once a people were born, lived and loved. They are gone now, leaving the remnants of their forgotten lives to rot and rust.

Some highways parallel the routes of the pioneers -- the 49ers, the Overland, the Oregon Trails. In a few places one can step a short distance from the paved roads and see the ruts left by the wagon wheels on their westerly treks to the distant promised land of California.

There are a few places on streets and roads that are sometimes called "haunted" or "magnetic hills." You stop your vehicle, turn off the motor, move the gears to neutral and release the brakes. The car then apparently rolls uphill. These are optical illusions so curious they have to be experienced to be believed. No spooks here, folks![1]

But there are certain stretches of roads that can indeed be termed "haunted." They can be active days, but more frequently at night. The specter of a human or animal appears in the roadway. The motorist takes to the ditch or hits a tree as the apparition vanishes. In many of these places the roads are straight ahead and free of obstructions. Law enforcement officers know them well for their frequency of accidents.

Other haunted roads display other types of strange phenomena. One is the inexplicable stoppage of automotive engines without apparent cause. Perhaps the most astonishing example of this kind of paranormal mischief was reported in the *New York Times,* Oct. 25, 1930. Forty automobiles stalled simultaneously on a haunted road in Saxony, Germany. Angry motorists had to wait for an hour before they could continue

---

1. For a list of magnetic hills, see *Curious Encounters,* by Loren Coleman, Faber and Faber, Boston, 1985.

their trips. Mysterious powerful "rays" directed by an unknown inventor was the only mundane explanation suggested.[2]

While on a motor trip from Indiana to New Orleans, one of the writers of this book once investigated a haunted road in a rural area near Tupelo, Mississippi, birthplace of Elvis Presley, the late singer and actor. This road had been abandoned years after a new shorter highway had been built eliminating curves. Strange occurrences along its route had been reported in journals devoted to psychic and bizarre events in the early 1930s.

It was said that all kinds of apparitions appeared along this road. Houses and outbuildings appeared and disappeared where such structures had never existed and now never would be built. One witness told of riding his horse through a herd of hogs, a type of livestock that had not been raised in the region for many years.

As I walked along the road, now little more than a path, I heard the birds singing in the trees and the myriad noises of insects in the weeds. It was a typical sunny summer day. No, I didn't see any herd of hogs. One cannot turn on paranormal events at will. The phenomena obeys its own laws of manifestation. I was simply enjoying my stroll.

Then I stopped. Something was wrong. Something had changed. Then I realized that I could no longer hear the birds singing or the hum and buzz of insects. An aura of profound silence surrounded me. I felt no fear, but I did feel apprehensive. I walked on and quite suddenly I heard the birds and insects. When I returned to the same place there was no envelopment of silence. The vortex had closed.

This happened years ago. Even then the roadway was vanishing with weeds growing between pieces of crumbling blacktop. It has probably totally disappeared by this time.

There are vortices, windows or aberrations from our physical plane to alternate realities, parallel realms or worlds that interpenetrate our own on different vibratory levels. There are places far more phenomenal than a lonely rural road in Mississippi.

Some students and writers suggest that these apertures may be the origin of many kinds of appearing and disappearing anomalies such as phantom cats, mysterious kangaroos and reports of big foot or sasquatch. Others theorize such openings may explain UFOs (unidentified flying objects) and similar appearances that are reliably witnessed, but later cannot be found.

Other of these interdimensional visions may be space-time warps giving observers glimpses of the past. This would explain the repeated

---

2. For other haunted road phenomena see *Weird America*, by Jim Brandon, E.P. Dutton, New York, 1978; also *Mysterious America*, by Loren Coleman, Faber and Faber, Boston, 1983.

visions of the Versailles Palace gardens as they existed in the time of Louis XVI and Marie Antoinette in France, the repeated re-enactment of the battle of Edge Hill in England, and the numerous accounts that can be found in psychic annals. Oriental philosophers say these visions are the Akashic Records, the earth memory.

Prospector Road is a haunted road in the gold rush country. The pavement and adjacent hills are over old mines, most of which have caved in. In a few the collapse of tunnels gave miners premature burials.

Prospector Road is a winding, half paved, often one lane path of a road which runs the seven mile stretch adjacent to the more traveled county built and maintained Marshall Road, constructed in 1957 to accommodate the ever increasing traffic. Marshall Road follows a narrow cliff from Lotus to Georgetown. Prospector, often called the "old road" having been utilized since it was built by Chinese labor in the 1800's, cuts the winding mountainside connecting with Marshall at both Lotus and Garden Valley. The barely traveled road and surrounding terrain has a history as colorful as any of the gold rush era. Because of the treacherous nature of the countryside, many a wagon and later automobiles over-turned, spilling their passengers down the hillsides to their death. A stagecoach stop, though moved to another site, is still visible on private acreage along Prospector Road. It was built as a half-way mark between Lotus and Garden Valley for the comfort of weary travelers. Later a line shack and check station were built along Prospector Road at the O'Brien and Maxwell Cromite Mines, both prosperous businesses, as cromite was a needed commodity during World War I for ammunition. The area produced one of the largest cromite finds, and the rock was often hauled by wagon down the winding path to Coloma, and then on to Placerville where it was shipped out by rail.

In the 1800's several lone miners made substantial gold discoveries in these hills, which account for its name. As with the age-old story of prospecting and claim jumping, many a miner who bragged a bit too openly about his "find" was strangely lost among the hills of Prospector, their bodies never recovered. It is suspected that many a spirit roams the Prospector hills, at least one still seeking the gold he never discovered while having his life cut short while trying.

Perhaps it was his specter who frightened a young couple with poltergeist-like pranks soon after they settled in a new home on Prospector Road. This is the story of Frank and Ruth Cooper.[3]

Late one night Ruth awakened from fretful slumber feeling cold and

---

3. Pseudonyms are used in this chapter by request. The persons involved, however, have signed affidavits testifying to the truth of their accounts. These affidavits are on file with the original interviews.

strangely apprehensive. She knew she had made a good fire in the wood-burning stove before retiring and the two-story cabin should still be warm. Still she felt something was wrong. Was there an intruder in the house? She awakened her husband and together they went down the stairs.

Frank had locked and bolted the front door earlier in the evening. Now it was ajar. The bolt pin remained in the outward position, yet the wall slot where it should still be secured had not been torn. They could find no evidence of forced entry.

Except for the mystery of the unexplained open door, everything appeared to be as it should. That is, except for the dog. Hearing a frightened yelp, they turned to find their pet huddled and trembling in a corner of the room. Ruth hugged her husband as they looked outside into the darkness. They could see nothing unusual. Thus was the family introduced to the ghost of Prospector Road.

This apparition is described by residents as attired in work clothing. To those who are able to see him, he appears semi-transparent, tall and craggy, sporting a beard. To those who cannot see him, he is a pesky, annoying trickster. Most folk believe his purpose is to keep people away from a claim he never recovered.

The Cooper cabin is in dense underbrush, barely visible from the road, and an ideal place to allow a dog to run at will. This was a deciding factor in the couple's decision to rent the cabin. The boxer, however, doesn't take advantage of his privilege. He refuses to go far from his owner's side, passing up each opportunity to corner a rabbit or chase a deer.

Frank and Ruth have observed the tall field grass spreading as if someone is walking through it when there is no one there. Occasionally they hear the sound of footsteps. At such times Buster will growl softly, wag his tail frantically, and cause the hairs on his back to bristle.

Not from their landlord, of course, but from the neighbors, the Coopers learned that former occupants of their cabin had hurriedly left the premises -- once in the middle of the night leaving their possessions behind. "We moved here because we like the country," Ruth said. "We often find dishes and other small objects moved around and sometimes something will be broken. Anyway, we have decided to stay here."

"At least until something really, and I mean really, disturbing happens," Frank added, glancing over his shoulder.

"Strange things have happened since we moved here," Ruth continued, "and the matter of the front door lock was only the first. One evening we heard the children shouting and banging on the door to their bedroom. When Frank and I investigated, we found that their door had been locked. From the outside! This was impossible, as the only other people in the house were Frank and myself. When this happened several times, Frank took the lock off. I figured this would be the end of the problem."

Ruth lit a cigarette with a somewhat shakey hand. "It wasn't though," she continued. "There was also an old-fashioned lock on the door. You know, the kind where you have to insert a key. Well, our landlord said he didn't know of the existence of the key, so not to concern ourselves with it. So one day the kids were locked inside their room, but this time an invisible key was turned by an invisible something. Maybe the ghost really likes the kids after all. Anyway, Frank removed the door, and the children will just have to make do with a doorless bedroom."

"The gun incident was the craziest," said Frank, gesturing into the air. "One evening when the children had all gone to friends' houses to spend the night, I did not bother to unload my .22 rifle. There was no one here who could get hurt with it, so I just propped it up against the front door for the night." He shrugged his shoulders the way one totally baffled would do. "When we got up the next morning and went downstairs, I found all the bullets next to the gun lying on the floor." He paused, frustrated. "Now, how is this possible?"

His neighbors feel the same way, although times can be trying. "I just want to know what causes all the commotion around here," said George, a man in his early 40's. "Something's amiss, unnatural, but we have lived with it so long it is beginning to seem normal to us. I guess it doesn't frighten me any more, but just when you think it is gone for good, something unheard of and inexplicable happens again!"

Little things like objects being moved around and strange noises could be tolerated, but last summer things came to a frightening crescendo.

"My son Billy and three of his friends had decided to take a walk just after dark," he began.

His son interrupted. "Why do things always have to happen to me? I never believed in ghosts, and I don't want to now," the seventeen-year-old, straight A student said. "But I have to. I saw him clearly, and so did my friends."

Billy's ghostly encounter happened on a warm summer's evening while his parents were entertaining several friends. Billy was occupied with companions of his own age, two who came along with their parents, and another who is a school chum. Soon the teenagers became bored with parental chatter, and excused themselves to take a walk down Prospector Road.

As all kids do, they needed a chance to vent their extra energy. Their walk consisted of laughing and joking, pushing each other into the bushes, and treating each other with casual lightheartedness, happy to be free of the regimented behavior expected of them while in the company of their parents. Billy took the lead, taking pride in parading his friends around an old shed, and then allowing them to explore the loft in the cattle barn. Afterward, by a criss-cross pattern, he led them back up the hill toward the road, to display his new baby lamb in the pen just beyond the house. But, as they turned the curve, Billy saw something shining in the moonlight. He instinctively put his arms out to stop his friends.

Billy and his buddies took a step backward, as a filmy outline, not of this world, materialized and faced them on the path. With the moonlight and dim light escaping from the back porch, they could see the figure of a tall man draped in tarp-like material which appeared to be a tattered rain garment. Whether the apparition heard the startled teenagers, or if he was to do so from some twisted coincidence of fate, the enraged swaying specter turned and glared fixedly at the boys.

"You cannot understand real fright until your eyes meet those of a ghost," Billy exclaimed, perspiration on his forehead. "We didn't know whether to run or stand still so that it wouldn't come after us. My biggest fear was that it would touch me."

The boys stood still as living tombstones, as the apparition pointed a finger at them, accusingly. Later upon separate interrogation, each boy was to confirm the same description and order of events. From Billy's own words, "It appeared his feet were not standing on the ground, but maybe a foot above. He swayed slightly from side to side. We couldn't really see through him, but there seemed to be a transparentness around his frame. He looked cold and wet, bluish in color, though the evening was hot, at least 85 degrees, and we had no rain in months. With his finger still pointed directly at us, he opened his mouth to say something we could not hear. He slowly, deliberately mouthed soundless words."

At this, one of the boys broke away, racing for Billy's house. Perhaps this broke the "spell", or perhaps because it was simply time, the unearthly vision turned, and floated down the embankment.

"When we told our parents, and we all went back to the spot where we had seen the ghost, we could find no trace of him. There were no footprints, broken twigs, nothing! We were really upset, and it took several hours for our folks to calm us down. All of my friends will admit to sleeping with the lights on for several nights."

The fright of the boys was doubtless genuine. Billy acquired temporary psychological problems. At the insistence of their parents, all of the boys went through counselling. Never did any of them deviate from their stories of the ghost and how they had observed him.

Of course, Billy's Dad has his own stories to tell.

"It wasn't very long ago that the tools disappeared," he said, looking at Billy who shook his head agreeing. "We had a shop in an old outbuilding on the property. Along the wall are hooks and shelves I erected to hold my tools. Well, one afternoon we made a commitment to some friends to go to Sacramento and help them work on their car. My son, a friend from the mountain, Dave, and I took the tools off the shelf, and making several trips to be certain we had everything, loaded them into

The Old Prospector

the back of my truck. We covered the tools with a tarp, went back into the house for a quick glass of water, and got into the truck to make our drive. Well, the punch line is, when we got to Sacramento, the tools were gone.

"I have to admit," the father told us, "I was upset and angry. How would you like to think that 400 dollars worth of tools had been stolen? I could only surmise that they had been taken when we stopped for a hamburger on the way. We had to call around to all of our friends and neighbors to gather up enough tools to get the job done."

"Luckily, I was insured," the man continued, "and as soon as we returned home, I intended to call my insurance agent. But it wasn't necessary," he added, a look of disbelief in his eyes. "When we returned to the house, the tools were all where they should be, in their proper spaces on the shelf, as if they had never been removed. Someone, or something, still as yet unknown to this world took them out of the truck. My God... that's spooky!"

"Then there is the other story about that shed, Dad," Billy was quick to remind his father. "The same shed has a lock that can only be hitched from the inside," his father said, taking up the story. "The shed has no windows, and only one door. This door has a lock and a key so it can be locked from the outside too, but sometimes when I am inside, and don't want to be disturbed, I will lock it from the inside. Well, one day we found the door locked from the inside. The lock is one of those with a bar across, not one that could trip up by itself. It would definitely take someone on the inside of the building to lock it. Yet when I called out, no one answered from inside. When Billy got home from school we broke the door down, taking half the door casing with it, to get back into the shed. I made Billy wait outside, and I went into the building with a gun, thinking perhaps a vagrant had gotten into it, actually not knowing what to think but there was no one inside. Not a trace of a person! Somehow the door was locked from the inside and without a way for whoever locked it to get back outside, that is impossible. It's simply impossible!"

Billy's father continued, thoughtfully. "This is the same shed," he said, "which was a stagecoach stop in the 1800's. We moved it to this site on our property. Do you think that could have something to do with the strange activity around here? Do you think moving the building might have upset the ghost?"

On a cold, blustery night about 10:30 p.m., a waitress returning from her job in Coloma drove the winding cliff on Marshall Road just above the area where the ghost had been seen on Prospector Road. The road was slick, the going slow. Wanting to get home as soon as possible, she had only rubbed the front windshield on the driver's side of the car clean enough of frost so that she could see. The rest of the windshield remained covered with ice. As she turned the curve which placed her car just above the area where the stagecoach stop rests below her, she heard a loud crash. On the passenger side of the windshield, imbedded in the frost, appeared the distinct outline of an outstretched hand and arm. She feared she must have hit someone, though the mountain road was deserted at this time of the night, certainly no person in their right mind would venture to walk it.

The driver pulled off to the side, taking out her flashlight. Trembling, she got out of her car, and searched the road and embankment for a body. There was none. She looked for fallen branches, anything that could have crashed into her windshield leaving the mark. Nothing! Shaking, she got back into her car, looking at the mark on the windshield. The hand and arm did not begin to fill with frost again until she reached her home, four miles away.

That same night, at approximately the same time, a strange voice was heard outside the young couple's cabin. They had seen the waitress' car lights ascending Marshall Road just above their house and the old stagecoach stop. As the family carried a final load of firewood from their truck into their cabin, the voice was heard distinctly. It said: "Stay away from my claim."

5

GARDEN VALLEY
Remnants of the Rosecranz Mine

As mining moved from the rivers and streams to the mountains, woods and canyons surrounding the American River, international developers from around the globe sent out 'scouts' to survey the country and report back the most logical places for gold to be found in the hills. Lode mines shot up with rapid regularity, and often ceased operation within months of their first conception. *The American Heritage Dictionary of the English Language,* New Dell Edition, First Printing July 1980, defines 'lode' as a vein of mineral ore deposited between layers of rock. Often a 'vein' would be found, and mines would appear within a quarter mile from the first mine, along the same vein, stretching for miles. Mines prospered, bringing many dollars to the small communities that popped up with familiar urgency. Others were abandoned, left to rot as gold seekers moved to richer ground.

Fall was in the air when in 1849 two men, George and Stephen Pierce, purchased a piece of land high above Coloma and planted a garden. As their garden prospered, they sold the vegetables to neighboring camps. When they sold their land, years later, they purchased another, in the same vicinity, and planted another garden. That one also prospered, yielding much more than they could ever use. Many folks became aware of the rich soil. The Pierce brothers sold their first property to the McConnell brothers, who changed the place into a trading post where they carried on the tradition and sold valuable vegetables. In 1852 the McConnell brothers provided all the vegetables for a 4th of July celebration, and in appreciation, then and there it was decided that this area, rich in soil, should be called Garden Valley. A post office was soon established, and Garden Valley became a town.

Little has changed Garden Valley over the years. It is still a small, lush garden community, peppered with pines and brush. Neighbors still wave to each other as they pass, as no one is a stranger. Sometimes the men folk sit around and talk about the good old days. Sometimes they talk about the ghosts.

Sitting on a hill, about 100 yards from the only major road that runs through this tiny and untouched town is one of the many old mines and outbuildings which still dot the hills in the gold-rush country. This one, for reasons forgotten through time, is called the Rosecrans(z). It is a nondescript mine, of cement and wood, originally three stories high, each year crumbling further courtesy of the rains and wind that come in fall and winter. The rotted base will give way soon, and the remaining Rosecranz will cease to stand, for indeed all things abandoned and forgotten cannot survive without proper care and maintenance. The Rosecranz is no exception.

The Rosecranz was not a very hearty producer in comparison to other mines in the area. Its major contribution was around the year 1888 when it produced $21,000 in gold ore that yielded $10 per ton. Originally worked to an inclined depth of 200 feet, the mine was reopened in 1936 and 1939, when it ceased operation for good. It was never recorded that any further substantial find was pulled from the earth surrounding the Rosecranz Mine.

If there was ever anything that set this mine apart from the others, it would be that as far back as the community can remember, strange sounds and lights have been seen permeating from the abandoned edifice. On still summer evenings banging can be heard, as if someone is still working the mine. Voices resound in busy laughter. Hammers pound invisible nails. When investigated, no one is there. Nothing has been moved or altered. No new footsteps are found in the dirt. No old timbers have fallen. A baffled community can find no answers to this strange and inexplicable phenomena, as many of the residents of the area continue to be frightened by the unknown.

One such incident involves two brothers, long-time residents of the area. The boys, aged 17 and 19, had recently moved into a home which exists along a long path through the woods, and next to the Rosecranz.

On a summer day in 1988 they took their dog for a walk along that path. The dog, a well-bred German Shepherd of little fear, strutted ahead of his masters, chasing birds and exploring the underbrush. It was a lazy day as many are in the gold-rush country, where the boys had no thought but to perhaps get a video and invite some friends over later in the evening. All was well with the world.

It was then that they heard it. The dog stopped in front of them, and not making a sound, refused to continue down the path. His fur raised on his back, and he looked at his masters for command. Should he attack? If so, what?....

The boys heard the sound of earth moving. "It was like something collapsing. Then we heard clanging and one loud bang," the older brother said excitedly. "I held my dog so he wouldn't go running off. We heard the sounds of someone working at that old abandoned mine," he said. "There

The crumbling Rosecranz Mine in Garden Valley. Strange sounds permeate these decaying walls, and cry out in the surrounding woodlands.

was hammering and voices. Then it all faded away, slowly getting softer until we couldn't hear it anymore." The younger brother fiddled with the lining of his jacket as he remembered what happened. "The dog seemed confused as to what was going on. We could see nothing strange, and yet there were these sounds. Something was happening, and yet it wasn't," he said.

In that split second, the dog did something he had never done before, and hasn't done since. "He put his tail between his legs and took off for home. We were happy to follow him!" the boy said.

"I have heard it too," stated a pretty 19 year old honor student from Garden Valley. "I also saw the light."

It seems that the mine displays a mysterious light which shows itself on many occasions, most predominantly in the fall. It is always elusive, hovering to the left side of the mine head and crasher section of the two-story building, and it appears to always be encased in an ectoplasmic fog.

The teenager was anxious to tell about her experience. "At a little past one a.m.," she began, "my friend Bob King and I were on our way home from a party. Some other friends were to have returned and picked us up, but they were detained, so because I had a curfew we had to walk. As we approached the mine we were startled by a loud crash inside the building. We stood in the shadows for a long time, quiet, just watching to see what it was. My heart was pounding as it was pretty dark there in the woods. Just as we were getting ready to resume our walk home, I thought I saw someone move in front of the window and there was an eerie light coming from the side of the building." She hesitated a moment, remembering, wanting to give a good and complete description. "The light was a misty white and it seemed to hover and glow. It was an oblong shape, and as I said, hovered. From side to side. Slowly!" She waited patiently for us to take notes. "Bob started throwing rocks at the mine, because we thought, well, we were hoping anyway, that someone was there playing tricks on us. If there was someone there, they would have been hurt by those rocks. No one answered, and there was obviously no one around. Bob took my hand and we ran the remaining half mile home. Later I learned that many people have seen the mysterious light at the Rosecranz Mine."

As if the ghostly mine, with all her inhabitants were not enough, the Rosecranz keeps another secret to herself.

The Rosecranz is also haunted by a voice in the night, a helpless soul whose screams plead for help from one of the many holes which are death traps today to the unsuspecting victim who does not know their whereabouts, or who ventures beyond the crude barb-wire fences erected haphazardly around the danger areas. In the community's laid back way, no warning signs have been erected, perhaps because the mine is now on private property, reason in itself to stand clear. Years ago open stopes were used, all along the old shaft, north and south of it, and the holes are filled with water and debris yielded by the forest over the years, which surround the mine. Perhaps this is the place from which this poor, helpless soul repeats its own horrible death, over and over again, year after year. What quirk of fate could decree such terrible punishment, and when and who can put the anguish to rest? It is a strange tale too as no mention in the archives or old newspapers could be found concerning a death from drowning at the Rosecranz. Many people disappeared at the time of the gold rush. We wonder which one, and who, is our suffering soul?

"It's eerie and strange," said Bob King, 21, who had another encounter while walking near the mine. A rock hound, he was looking at the ground when he heard the voice of someone close by.

"I heard a frantic 'help', a mumbled voice as if drowning, and then coming up for air," King shuddered as he told the story. "I ran to the only spot that was close that I knew was a hole in the ground, and the one from which direction I had heard the voice." He quietly remembered the unthinkable. "There could have been no one drowning in that hole. At least not then. The murky water in the hole had not been disturbed as was evident in the residue that was still intact on the top.

"Again I heard the cries of a man drowning...going down and down again, into that hole...." he remembered well. "It happened again, louder, and it sounded like a man fighting for air. I called out 'where are you?' not really wanting a reply, because deep down I knew what I had heard was not normal, the sound of someone actually in trouble right now, today. It sounded too distant, too strange." He looked up thoughtfully. "I needn't have worried. There was no reply. In fact, the forest was completely silent, not even a cricket could be heard. I started to leave, but was increasingly aware of the leaves rustling under my feet because of the strange silence. I stood still for what seemed a long time, but was probably just a minute or two. Slowly the sounds of birds, bugs, leaves, normal forest sounds came back. Activity returned. I swear to you, not so much as a leaf fell to the ground when the voice was there. I was never so glad as when I reached the road, the sun hit my face, and I heard the sound of cars coming in my direction. Civilization!" He thought for a minute, then spoke softly. "I have yet to go back, but one day I will. It will be with friends though. I won't go alone!"

It is certain this mine, of little other consequence, will be remembered as one of personality, and one that will refuse to die as even the last timber falls to the earth and the last metal roofing plank is stolen by some industrious rancher eager to build his own new barn at the expense of history. The Rosecranz is haunted. By whom, by what, and why, we do not know.

6

GREENWOOD
A Mystical Menagerie

Greenwood, in the heart of the Gold-Rush country, is a forlorn, strange town with a history of faded dreams. It has been called the town that time forgot. This is Greenwood today: a few scattered houses, a printing shop for a monthly newspaper, a family restaurant, a small post office, a padlocked schoolhouse abandoned since 1952 and the inevitable tavern where the patrons lie to each other about the day's activities.

It also has a collection of ghosts that occasionally appear in the streets, buildings, and around the site of a hanging tree. Its pioneer cemetery is haunted by the images of unhappy people whose bones lie in weed covered, sunken graves below shattered monuments.

It was not always so. In the middle 1800's, Greenwood was considered one of the more prosperous gold rush communities. It is situated above and between the South Fork and the Middle Fork of the American River making the location ideal for the army of gold panners who used the route through Long Valley (later named Greenwood Valley) to find their way to the American River.

In the winter when the river rose and made panning difficult, thousands of miners camped on higher ground and in the surrounding hills to search for the elusive metal with pick, shovel and chisel, waiting for the water to subside. For their supplies and recreation, they came to Greenwood. At that time the town boasted 14 general stores, a brewery, two theaters, a large hotel, and a half dozen saloons.

It was a time of hard but often rewarding labor, a time of blasted hopes, of rough justice, and earthly pleasures. It was a time when people faced daily the fundamentals of existence, the frustrations of life and its simple joys.

Many believed the overland railroad would pass through the valley. Alexander Bayley had faith in the rumor. Not far from Greenwood he built a three-story, brick mansion with the fortune he had earned in the gold fields. It would be an inn with a tavern, rooms for guests and his own luxurious home. It had Colonial porticoes and was backed with a terraced garden. Bayley opened the house with a grand ball on May 15, 1862, a date the old timers remembered. But Bayley had guessed wrong. His remaining years were bitter ones alone in his crumbling mansion.

In his booklet *Greenwood California, A Town That History Almost Forgot,* Leonard M. Davis writes: "History has not been kind to Greenwood. Little more than a phrase or two appears in such prestigious, multi-volumed works as Bancroft or Hittell, and Sioli's *El Dorado County History* has not considered the town worthy of more than two or three brief paragraphs."

Fire, the red menace that threatened so many Gold Rush towns with their lack of fire fighting equipment, repeatedly struck Greenwood. Four times it destroyed most of the business buildings in the community.

The last blow came in 1972 when a realigning of Highway 193 between Auburn and Georgetown bypassed Greenwood completely. Today the town is not even marked on many maps. Now its fate is close to complete oblivion.

Greenwood's genesis began in the summer of 1848 when mountain man Caleb Greenwood and his half-breed son, John, arrived in the valley from Coloma. They built a cabin and began seeking gold, but soon decided there were more profitable ways to make a living. Caleb decided to hunt deer instead of color and began supplying the growing army of hungry argonauts with venison. John and his wife, a half-breed French girl, opened a trading post.

Four years before Caleb Greenwood came to the site of the town that was to bear his family name, he performed a feat so incredible that he would always be a hero in the annals of the western Mountain Men. One can stand there today where it happened and look at the rocky precipice with utter astonishment. It is testimony to the dedicated determination of these early pioneers to reach California.

Greenwood was a Kentuckian who left the Daniel Boone country as a young man, married an Indian woman and fathered several hearty sons. In the spring of 1844 he joined the Stevens-Murphy Party of covered wagons and soon became its leader. From the prairies of Illinois the caravan began its long westerly trek -- oxen plodding, wheels turning, mile after mile. They were men with bronzed skin and wind-burned faces. They were women with rugged characters who faced daily hardships with boundless resourcefulness. There were days and nights of chilling cold, rain and damp misery, and times of relentless sun and scorching heat.

Across the Midwest, the Great Plains, and over Rocky Mountain passes, the train of wagons rumbled along until at last they reached the Sierra Nevadas, the final great barrier before the promised land. Part of the trail had been the same general route that would be followed two years later by the tragic Donner Party, past the location where Reno would someday be built, skirting what would later be named Donner Lake.

The Donner Party met its tragic fate when it took the Hastings Cut-off from the main trail and was trapped in the high mountains by early season blizzards and deep snow. The caravan broke up and the various groups, facing starvation, were forced to eat bark, twigs, hides, and finally the bodies of their dead. The suffering the party members endured is almost beyond belief.

Eventually the Stevens-Murphy Party, led by Greenwood, began following the special trail blazed by Edwin Bryant with eight companions. However, they had penetrated the mountains on horseback with a train of pack mules. They were unencumbered by large, heavy wagons loaded with women, children and household possessions.

Bryant, in his journal of his California trip, had been astonished at their "cyclopean magnitude, the... apparently regular and perfect... construction of its walls, turrets, and bastions."

The Stevens-Murphy Party struggled up the steep slope of the eastern side of the Nevadas only to come to a halt when faced by an almost perpendicular wall of granite rising about 12 feet in height. Old Caleb Greenwood gazed defiantly at the obstruction.

"We're not turning back to try to find another trail," he told his fellow travelers. "It's November. Too late in the year to go back. Soon the storms and snow will come. Come hell and high water, we are going to get through these damn mountains right here."

Greenwood circled the rock until he found a narrow crevice. Under his direction, the men in the party went to work chopping steps up the crevice. When the task was completed, the wagons were emptied. Some of the household goods were carried up the crevice piece. The heavier articles were hauled up by ropes held by men and women standing on top of the rocky precipice.

Next came the oxen. They were half pushed, half dragged, with men below and ropes above the crevice. Now came the challenge of the wagons. Parts of several wagons were removed to serve as levers, one by one. At the top of the rock six or eight ox teams pulled as men and women below used all their group strength to lift. Wheels turned as the wagons rolled up the face of the cliff.

With grim determination and inconceivable labor, several other barriers scarcely less difficult were conquered in the same way. There was no high water, but the repeated frustrations could have been considered hellish.

Nevertheless, Caleb Greenwood brought his caravan to the valleys of California and became a legend among the legendary western Mountain Men.

When gold was discovered at Sutter's sawmill in January, 1848, the ever restless Greenwood happened to be near Coloma. Several months later he and his son were panning for color in the American River not far away. They were soon joined by hundreds of avid miners. Panning was hard, tedious work. More rapid and greater wealth could be gained by serving the gold seekers. So Greenwood went deer hunting and his son opened his trading post.

Fog hovered over the old pioneer cemetery the evening we drove to the half-hidden grounds. Only the tops of the larger tombstones could be seen above the weeds in an eerie disarray, broken and worn, mute reminders of another day, another time.

Despite the passage of so many years and the crumbling abandonment of this long forgotten graveyard, there was enough testimony among Greenwood's inhabitants to warrant our visit. It seems there was a secret hidden here over a century old. It could only manifest at times as a wraith with an aura of sorrowful frustration. We came with feelings of sympathy. We were there to do what we could.

To make a thorough investigation, we decided on taking a seasoned professional psychic sensitive with us. She and the authors arrived at the cemetery at the same time. We had chosen her for integrity and ability. As writers on psychic phenomena, we wanted the best in expertise to aid in a possible exorcism and transition. This psychic presented fine credentials and an excellent track record. We had the professional ability to know an imposter when we worked with one, and she was not one of them. We were an honest team.

Sharon Turner was our gifted psychic. A graduate of the Berkeley Psychic Institute, she has a ministerial degree and a B.A. from Sonoma (California) State University. For 15 years she has given advanced spiritual development and aura readings. She has a number of prominent clients.

After the usual formalities, we followed Turner the length of the cemetery. We observed the tombstones overgrown with weeds and brush. We fondled the granite and wood mementoes of loved ones so long gone, feeling the sorrow of those they left behind. So many were of youngsters six months old, two years old. The devastation felt by those mothers of long ago lingered on in our hearts as well. The memories of wives who lost their husbands, of men who lost whole families. The pain still remains as it does in all cemeteries, through the years.

We had heard the stories local teenagers tell of a ghost in this long forgotten graveyard. Imaginations can run rampant with the help of a few beers, and a curious word spoken from a friend. The teenagers told of a phantom strong enough to topple an unsuspecting spectator, showing his presence to the wide eyed nonbelieving machos only in the graveyard to prove their bravery to their beautiful girlfriends.

As authors we investigated the tale as a possible story for our book, but we took this mission for another reason as well. We are both history lovers, wishing to preserve all that is left of a heritage so important to

American Lore. This small cemetery, hidden and old, should be protected from the vandals and curiosity seekers who would make a mockery of it. Since the story of a ghost in the cemetery began, the area had been looted, vandalized, and strewn with litter. We investigated to see if there actually was a ghost. If true, proper precautions could be taken to protect the cemetery. If not, perhaps the rumor could be laid to rest.

We didn't have to wait long. The hair rose on our arms as the psychic proclaimed, "I feel it. Its here! Yes, there is an entity, the kids are not just telling stories."

We watched as Taylor's breathing labored, something that often happens in the presence of spirits. Though the authors did not see the ghost in this instance, we can ascertain that it was there by the heaviness in the air, and the sudden quiet stillness of the air as cold enveloped our bodies. Unseen fingers caressed our arms and held our fingers. Turner was quick to identify the spirit as that of a man.

"The ghost the children see is that of a man," she told us. "He is searching for someone called Lana. Yes, he is strong enough to be seen by many people, and can, at times, move things when atmospheric conditions allow. He is searching, yes, worried, about this child Lana. He cannot find her......."

Turner felt the weight of the illness that was to take the life of this entity. "He feels deep pain as in arthritis," she said, hunching over, anticipating his pain. "It runs through both his hands, to his neck and spinal column. This man died of this pain, coupled with an illness of fever and intestinal flu. In life he was not able to express sadness, sorrow or emotion. He feels badly for this."

It was getting dark and we chose to resume our work with this old spirit the following day. Turner spoke to the entity, explained that she would try to release him from his earthly state at that time.

As we left the cemetery, all going to our protective homes, little did we know that the anxious ghost would not wait. Another amazing fact was learned that night. A spirit can leave its established "haunting" place, and travel wherever it needs to go if it so desires. In this case, it followed Turner home.

The spirit did not forget the promise. Apparently after all the years of being earthbound, it was not willing to wait another day to leave this good earth. About 2 a.m. that same evening, the restless specter appeared at Turner's bedside, startling her husband, a man not likely to embrace the world of the unknown. He saw a man, tall and slender with large hands standing at the side of their bed. When the entity reached out to touch him, he was not amused. He woke his wife with one hurried shake. As she sat up in bed, the lights in the house flickered off and on three times. Her husband quickly left the room and slammed the door behind him.

Turner knew what she must do.

As our psychic later explained to us, she used her ability to create a pathway of light that connects the earth plane to the heavenly plane. In her final act of releasing the spirit, she removed the plight that had kept this poor man from seeking his just reward. He stepped into another world. "A healing took place that is eternal," she said. "He entered a world he should have entered a hundred years ago." The confirmation came. The lights of her home again flickered off and on. Three times. "He is at peace now," Turner feels.

The next day, through records, we were to learn that an early resident of Greenwood had a daughter, Alana, who died at the age of three months, just two months after her father's demise. If he was our spirit, he is now, hopefully, with Alana, his worry lifted.

The Mother Lode is full of ghosts from the past. Two weeks after the release of this spirit, local officials were alerted to the same cemetery by several frightened spectators who testified to seeing a ghost of a man during the hours of 10:00 and 11:30 p.m. Since that eventful night, other reports of ghosts have come from the cemetery. One often seen specter is of a man with a bandana stretched across his forehead, and wearing a long waistcoat. He appears to be floating among the tombstones. Perhaps caretakers should be hired, day and night, to protect the cemetery -- from the living.

But back downtown the quaint old building that now houses R & B Associates, the monthly newspaper the "Greenwood Flea," was once, if rumor serves correct, a mortuary, the back portion of the building being rented to a coffin maker. Actually, to be fair and correct, we must say we refer to an identical building to the one that now inhabits R.B. Associates. The original burned to the ground in the 1800's. The current building, a "dead" ringer of the former, was built in the 1920's. Buildings were used for many purposes over the years, and if the structure was not used as a mortuary, the elder Greenwoodites certainly missed a great opportunity, considering the official Greenwood "hanging" tree is right outside. In the 1800's many a poor soul was laid out in the front room facing the street, the body in the coffin tilted at one of the two windows to be viewed from outside. Several hangings took place during Greenwood's heyday, most notably that of a James Graham in 1851, a denizen from Baltimore who on a hunting trip with a Mr. Lesley, got angry with his companion, and shot him full of buckshot. Lesley, left for dead, stumbled to a cabin owned by Tom Birch, who just happened to be the Constable. He spilled his fate moments before he died. Graham was apprehended and stood trial. A jury found him guilty of the deed and hung him from the famed oak. Another murder occurred a few years later in 1854 when a Samual Allen murdered an old gentleman as he tended his garden. No one knows the reason Allen chose to do in the elderly William Shay, but apparently the aged fellow made him very angry because not only did he knock him down but after the deed was done, he repeatedly stomped the man's head into the ground.

Unfortunately for Allen, there was an eye witness, Antonio Dias, who told the justice. Allen was ordered to stand trial in Coloma, but while being transported an unruly crowd decided to alter the route, and headed for the same Greenwood hanging tree.

Liverpool Jack, another character of uncertain respectability was to find his fate at the end of the Greenwood hangin' tree, after almost escaping with the crime of murdering his partner. Known only as "the Frenchman," Jack's partner made the unpardonable sin of confiding to Jack that he had found astounding amounts of gold. Jack killed him then and there. To cover his tracks, he told the constable he had witnessed two blacks "splitting open" his partner's head. Though the two black men were taken into custody, they were soon released for insufficient evidence.

Both our relentless constable Tom Birch, and the powerful justice Sam Crane were shrewd men. They ordered both black men and Jack secretly trailed. Within a few months Jack was spotted at a horse race in Coloma, spending some of the Frenchman's new-found fortune. He dangled from a rope at the Greenwood Tree.

But back to the building. The present occupants, printers by trade often stay up late at night proofreading copy and meeting an inevitable deadline. Strangely, they rarely notice occurrences that would terrify persons not quite so hearty.

Among the other ghosts who have been seen enough times in and around Greenwood for us to consider credible, is that of a woman considered to have been a prominent member of the community in the 1800's. She is always in the company of a young boy of about seven years of age. She has strong convictions about right and wrong, and is often seen at the foot of the hanging tree. She has been heard telling the boy that a man who is hanging was not "Godly" and that is why he has been put to death in this fashion. She was apparently a woman who kept things stirred up in her day, and took charge of everyone's business as well as her own. She has a sternness about her, a strictness, and it is believed many people of her day were afraid of her. Possibly she refuses to leave Greenwood because of her control level of energy. She continues to try and take charge of everything that happens in Greenwood. She has been seen, along with the boy, entering the door of R & B Associates.

Some passing-by motorists at night see the outline of a man hanging from the Greenwood hanging tree. Turner insists the entity is still hanging because he cannot get past the death experience. "He does not want to give up the body for something that he did not do," she says. "The man was hung and he was innocent."

There is the spirit of a man who had a problem with alcohol. He was a part-time gold miner, a thin gentleman, who panned when he needed the money for a drink. He would be seen staggering through town, a bottle in his hand.

There is the energy of a gold miner with the name of Duke who still frightens the occasional visitor to Greenwood. This man apparently was very jolly as he walked through the streets of Greenwood with a little dog at his side. He will, on occasion, try to show off his boots to startled onlookers. There is also the ghost of a tall, skinny, bespectacled man, racing through the buildings with papers in his hands. He is not dressed as a miner, but as a prosperous merchant. It is not certain if he was a newspaper man, or an attorney. Local folk like to sip a brew and contemplate the issues.

So if you are in the area, why not take a stroll through this tiny block-long country town. Maneuver your way through the cattle which have an uncanny way of breaking through fences to stand in the streets, and place yourself in front of R & B Associates, the hanging tree, or the old Greenwood cemetery. It could be an experience you will never forget.

7

GEORGETOWN
The Ghosts Up The Hill

Traveling eight miles from Greenwood, uphill, you will come to the town of Georgetown, and experience a village that could not care less about conventionality. Georgetown is still untouched in spirit (excuse the pun) as an 1800's town. Naturally there are those bullheads who try to clean 'er up, bring a conversion to modern day life. Unfortunately, as in most cases, this is done for the sake of making a buck, and at the expense of a beautiful past. What they might not know is, Georgetown won't go down easy for the count. Nothing runs by the book in Georgetown, and if you think I'm lying, ask any sheriff who patrols the county, or any official who tried to stop folks from parking their cars in the middle of the road when they couldn't find a conventional parking place. We all know that change is inevitable, but we salute the rednecks and old-timers who fight for their rights and way of life, resist change, and remain individuals among many. God love them!

One of the authors will never forget her first experience in this town. I just happened to go into the Georgetown Hotel and Bar to cure an angry thirst. What a surprise for a city girl doing research for a book. On the floor was sawdust strewn with peanut shells.

Were there no health laws here? Sitting under tables, in a corner of the room, and, as I remember, one on a stool at the bar next to his master, were a variety of man's best friends. Hound dogs, labs, shepherds, mutts, all sipping spilled beer and chewing nuts. Cowboys with long beards and cowgals with leather boots sat or danced, all with a drink in hand, all oblivious to this strange outsider in polyester slacks and high-heeled shoes. I remember a friendly whistle as I came in, thankfully, it put me at ease. I had yet to hear the stories of shootings and fights with outsiders, some exaggerated, some not. I was sized up and thought to pose no threat.

As I sat at my table and adjusted my purse, a lone horseman came through the swinging doors into the bar on his horse. The animal knew exactly where to go as he moseyed up to the bar, and the bartender knew what the horseman wanted as he drew a well beer and handed it to him in a mason jar. A swig of the brew, a swipe at his mouth with his sleeve, and, jar in hand, the horseman left from where he came, continuing down Main Street dodging cars. I finished my Manhattan, slipped off my shoes, and ordered a brew. I was hooked on Georgetown.

Georgetown is believed to be the source of the ever-familiar rumor that gave California the reputation of having streets paved with gold. The town was originally called Growlersburg as the nuggets mined were so large (often ten ounces or more). Miners called them growlers, claiming that they made a growling noise when swirled around in the pans. Nuggets were often found under the roots of trees, under rocks after storms, and in all the rivers, streams and gulches. There are stories of settler women digging holes to plant store bought rose bushes, only to find a nugget big enough to buy a complete garden.

Georgetown sprang up, as many did, a mining town around 1849. Upward of 2,000 nuggets were reportedly found within its hills, and between ten and twenty-five thousand miners made their way from the American River to take their chances in Georgetown.

As with mining settlements in the Mother Lode, Georgetown was ravaged by fire over and over again. In an effort to stop the flow of flames, in 1852 the town laid out one-hundred-foot wide streets to serve as fire breaks. Unfortunately their efforts did little to protect the business district as fires destroyed the town. During one fire in 1897 the flames swept through Main Street, reaching a cache of miners' dynamite, spewing debris as far away as two miles. True to their still determined nature, residents rebuilt as fast as the fire cooled, time and time again. Since the beginning of Georgetown, there has been a Georgetown Hotel, built, and rebuilt, after each devastating fire. This century-old hotel on Main Street is old and worn, with a downstairs bar and restaurant, and upstairs rooms for rent. Some still have iron beds and muslin curtains. Bath and showers are down the hall, and it is more a place to absorb atmosphere than to enjoy luxuries. Such are the ways of Georgetown.

Of all the ghosts, goblins, spooks and phantoms in the Mother Lode, there is one you won't want to miss when in the area -- the one that lingers in the Georgetown Hotel.

Georgetown Hotel

Folks at the Georgetown Hotel tell me that it is the only hotel in the United States that boasts of having a room 13. They may not be superstitious, but room 13 has a ghost residing inside. And, the elusive ghost roams the rest of the building when he is bored. He especially likes the cluttered kitchen. It is deeply suspected that the unknown specter is the remains of a previous owner who died in one of the major holocausts to beset early Georgetown, probably the 1897 fire which whipped through the town, destroying everything in its path.

The Georgetown Hotel. Upstairs is for lodging, downstairs is a tavern. Very informal, it is a cowboy bar out of the 1800's. It is haunted by a former owner

Cooks at the hotel have mentioned seeing him numerous times, out of the corner of their eyes, standing in the kitchen or by the heater in the bar. "He usually has his hands on his hips as if analyzing the place," they told the authors. "He is an older man, perhaps fifty years of age, tall and with salt and pepper colored hair. He has a pipe in his mouth. Sometimes when I go to the kitchen in the morning," one of the chefs told us, "things will be rearranged. I will have to go looking for pots and pans, spatulas and such. Being the last one to leave the night before, and having locked up myself, I know no one else could have done it. Then I look up, and he is there, staring at me. I blink my eyes, and he is gone. My heart does a double take. It is frightening, and a big annoyance."

According to Bobbie Thompson, former co-owner of the hotel, in an article written by this author for the *Georgetown Gazette* in 1983, "The television set downstairs will go on by itself in the middle of the night, and lights will go on and off without reason.

"Apparently the old gentleman had a small dog," said Thompson, "because he has also been seen." When redecorating the building, after pulling off layers of wallpaper Thompson came across a letter written in the 1800's to the now deceased owner, from his girlfriend expressing her feelings in having to leave him because of the death of her mother in another town. He burned to death before her return.

Another cook at the hotel told us, "I was working alone in the kitchen one night, when the locked freezer door flung open. When I turned around, I noticed that the garbage had been moved. I yelled out because I thought someone was playing a joke on me, but indeed, the building was empty. When I turned around to return to the kitchen, I saw a man standing there. I said, 'Okay, enough is enough!' but then he disappeared. I ran from the building."

Several other strange and eerie things have happened to this person while working in the Georgetown Hotel. Twice in one week she locked the door upon leaving for the night, and was puzzled to find it wide open when she returned the next morning. Nothing was missing from the premises.

Apparently when the ghost is upstairs he prefers to stay in room 13. Guests who have stayed in that room complained of weird and strange noises, bumps and crashes in the night. One woman complained of someone, or something, unseen sitting on her feet. "They were frozen," she said. "There was enough pressure for perhaps a small dog, or animal, to have sat down on them. After much shuffling of my legs, I was finally able to fling it off."

"Another strange thing happened a few winters ago," stated Jack White, Thompson's business partner, thoughtfully. "Bobbie and I heard something at the front door. It had snowed the night before, and the drifts against the door were at least two feet high. We wondered who could have made their way up to it. When we opened the door, we were astounded! We found deer tracks coming up to the door, but there was no deer. Stranger still, there were no deer tracks going the other way showing that he had turned around and left! It was as if the deer came up to the door, and disappeared into thin air! Now, what do you think of that?" he asked, as if wanting an explanation.

In the last few years in this rambunctious hotel, a man shot himself through the foot at the bar, an angry boyfriend shot his girlfriend through the hip in a jealous rage, and many in the bar have clapped their hands approvingly at the clanging bell which is suspended by a string at the ceiling, attached to a bed upstairs destined to go off each time the bed moves. But none of these events are as exciting as the sightings of the tall, dark ghost of the Georgetown Hotel. The authors don't have the answers for Jack White, but these haunted hills do seem to have their secrets. Be aware if you pass the Georgetown Hotel this Halloween and see someone in costume not asking for tricks or treats. You just might have encountered the Hotel Ghost!

American River Inn

An abrupt intruder haunts Room 5 of the American River Inn in downtown Georgetown, yet surprisingly, he rarely has a frightening effect on those who have seen him. His appearance is certainly adverse to his

The American River Inn, Georgetown
It is haunted by a craggy miner and his woman of the evening.

tender nature. But he loves three things -- honeymooners or happy lovers, Room 5 of the Inn, and his long-dead girlfriend, for whom he is still searching. Rumor tells us he last saw her in Room 5.

In its time the American River Inn was known as the American Hotel, and before a series of owners, name changes, and rebuildings because of the fires that have caused widespread havoc through Georgetown, was constructed over a productive lode known as the Woodside Mine. From the Woodside Mine, many pound-sized chunks of gold were extracted. At one point as much as $90,000 was pulled from the earth within two weeks. Many miners lost their lives in the shallow mines and tunnels of Georgetown. There are believed to be some still buried under the American River Inn, when that mine collapsed. A basement wall hides the grim story. Oscar survived that catastrophe. Such begins the tale of Oscar, our honeymoon ghost.

He was a hearty soul of the 1800's, a miner looking for a fortune like thousands of others at this time in history. He must have made an impact on the townsfolk, as his name is synonymous with Georgetown even to this day. Old timers tell tales about Oscar. He is remembered by stories passed down through generations as a gruffy old polk, about 5'8", ambitious and anxious to find his fortune. If there was a strike, Oscar was the first to pick up a shovel. He was fearless of the rickety mine shafts, and tapped off river channels. He was once known to be lost for several days in an extensively channeled, abandoned mine. When he did emerge, with the cheering of the crowd (who had been diligently looking for him), his first words spoken were a disgusted, "Didn't find no gold!" Such was his self-programmed thinking. But he had a perpetual romantic heart, and was to give his, foolishly or not, to a nameless "woman of the evening."

Now there was a time our beautiful American River Inn was not as luxurious as it is today, and a time when it was used for other types of guests than those the management caters to now. As we said before, miners had needs and in Georgetown they were often met at the American Hotel. As the tale goes, Oscar fell hard for a gold-rush prostitute. He was well aware of her occupation, in fact, it was how they met. Many years her senior, he was smitten enough to dream of making her his wife. They had long talks, before and after lovemaking. She told of missing her family in the east, and of making enough money to return there.

Whether the story is true, or if it is all conjecture, we cannot know for certain, but the ghost of the American River Inn certainly takes on all appearances and characteristics of the seemingly immortal Oscar. And, because we all have to die, Oscar found his demise suddenly one day, just above the Woodside Mine he once worked.

He had taken a job as a carpenter on the property, perhaps to be near his love. History shows he was very jealous of her. A heckler, a former 'client' of his girlfriend, insisted on belittling her name. Words were passed between the men. A scuffle prevailed, and in the heated moments that followed, the aggressor shot Oscar dead, on the steps of the American Hotel. His body died, but his spirit remained.

"The activity seems to be centered around the top of the stairs, and Room 5," stated Carol La Morte, who along with her husband Neal and owners Wil and Maria Collin purchased the American Hotel in 1984 as a family project, and embarked on the biggest challenge of their lives. They renamed the hotel the American River Inn, and for three long and painful months, remodeled, added eight bathrooms, reconstructed old woodwork and paneling, chose wallpaper reminiscent of the gold-rush era, and all in all, changed a declining fortress into a once again stately mansion. "Room 5 was in especially bad shape," she was to tell us, and which was evident from the photographs of before and after she was eager to show us. "Besides the bad shape, we began to feel uncomfortable working in the room. We were cold on a hot day. Something would brush past us, we could physically feel it, but no one was there. There was a 'presence' in that room as we worked it, but because the other members of our family did not want to admit to a 'ghost' I tried to concentrate on other aspects of what it could be. Obviously, since we have been admitting guests into that room for overnight stay, and they have actually seen a ghost, we have got to admit that he is here. And, what's interesting, is that very few of our guests are terrified of him, though he is gruff looking. He is a friendly ghost, who smiles at the lovers, and walks through the room as if he belongs there. He especially takes pride in appearing to honeymoon guests, as if he wants to be a part of their happiness."

Guest bear this out. A statesman who wishes to remain anonymous told the authors, "When we married, my wife and I stayed in Room 5 of the American River Inn. At 3:00 a.m., a man dressed in old, tattered clothes walked through the closed door from the outside balcony and into our room. Our light switched on for no reason, and he smiled as he continued walking through the closed door that leads to the hall. We both heard his footsteps seemingly go down the stairs to the main part of the house but I must admit, neither of us got out of bed to check this out. Our light then went back off. When I turned the light knob, it went back on because the lamp had been turned off the whole time." La Morte admits to us, and through affidavits, that electricians have been called to fix the problem, but to no avail. They now shrug their shoulders and say there is no possible electrical reason for this annoying fiasco.

The guest book at the American River Inn makes interesting reading. One couple, from Crestline California wrote in April of 1986, "We loved experiencing the comfort and romance of your beautiful Inn. Pam enjoyed feeling Oscar in our room and maybe she'll be able to sleep at our next stop in Ione!" On July 13, 1986, another guest wrote: "We already made reservations for next time. Long 'live' Oscar!" On November 9, 1986, a couple from Yuba City, California wrote: "The highlight of our visit was a visit from Oscar. In the wee hours our lamp went on for no reason. We're sure it was Oscar!"

Help at the Inn often experiences his presence when cleaning the room. La Morte admits to "talking to him when I know he is around so I won't get afraid." Several guests have told the management, "We were snug in our bed when this dirty looking miner type walked into the room, smiled at us, and left through the door." Oscar always enters through the door that opens up on the balcony, and leaves through the door at the top of the stairs. It makes no difference if the door is open or shut, he does not take time to fiddle with it.

"And, he has an uncanny way of whispering your name," La Morte was to admit to us. "Several guests complain of hearing their name spoken and no one is there." A letter received by the Inn written by guests from Hawaiian Gardens, CA states in part, "That evening at cheese and wine my husband and I were talking to each other. We learned that both of us felt uncomfortable each time we passed a specific part of the house. We compared notes and came to the conclusion that this is (must be) the house. I would appreciate any information...."

During a stay on June 23, 1986, a couple from Garden Valley, CA told of hearing a woman's voice as well as a man's in Room 5 of the Inn.

Because it is not publicized the owners have kept the ghost a secret, so none of the guests had prior knowledge that anything should be different about their stay. "We had just built our home and were celebrating by staying in the elegant Inn," the husband, a maintenance supervisor for the Roads Department of El Dorado County told the authors. "In the middle of the night I awoke to a whisper near my pillow. When I sat up, it was gone. Figuring I was just dreaming, I laid my head back down. Immediately the whisper was back. I heard a man in the background, but though I could not quite make out what they were saying, it was a woman's voice I heard distinctly. Then, I heard footsteps going down the stairs. The American River Inn is a great place, and I had one of the oddest experiences of my life in Room 5. I will never forget it."

And because a woman's voice is also sometimes heard from the depths of the unknown inside the Inn, it is interesting to note that soon after Oscar's death, a beautiful woman of the evening was to attire herself in her finest negligee, and, liquor in hand, take the leap of death from the balcony of the American Hotel. The doctor said her neck was broken instantly. Could it be a broken heart preceded it?

8

PLACERVILLE
Hangtown's Haunting Hangman

Main Street Placerville seems to house a ghost, and by lucky coincidence it's a stop you will probably already have on your agenda if you're looking for information: the Chamber of Commerce building! Over the past 15 years, employees at the building were grateful when Placerville city police responded to their calls. They were quite rightly "spooked" by the slightly transparent man with whiskers and top hat lingering in the balcony of the building.

Formerly called Hangtown because of the unusual number of hangings, lynchings and public executions, Placerville was founded in 1849 by a pair of prospectors lucky enough to have lined their pockets with $17,000 after one week's digging in this vicinity. Along with instant wealth came frontier justice. Many a man even suspected of jumping a claim found his life dangling at the end of a rope. So lucrative was the hanging business, the town had its official hangman, ready and prepared to pull the string, or whip the horse, under the unwilling victim. Historians tell us the most popular hanging tree, and later scaffoldings, were on the site of the Chamber of Commerce Building.

According to Marian Watry, former General Manager of the El Dorado Chamber of Commerce, and who worked in the building for many years, the ghost was often seen in the mezzanine which has now been covered over by a dropped ceiling to allow for lighting accommodations. "The building is old, and would sometimes creak," she told us. "One could certainly suspect that there was someone unseen there. What is interesting to me, is that in 1981 and 1982, when we remodeled the interior of the building, we experienced strange occurrences. Every time that workmen came in to renovate the building, the plumbing would stop up. Plumber after plumber was unable to locate the problem, but each time the workmen would go away, the problem disappeared. I hope our ghost is not unhappy that we remodeled the building. All in all, the building has a friendly feeling to it. It's strange, but sometimes, when I was looking for a certain paper or something, it would suddenly appear in front of me a short time later. Could this be the work of our ghost? If so, he does seem to be benevolent and friendly. He just didn't want the building to be changed or updated."

The county's historical Georgetown and *El Dorado Gazette* newspaper once shared the upstairs portion of the age-old structure with the Chamber of Commerce. The employees had their eyes and ears open for any unusual noises, tappings, or supernatural apparitions. The eerie inhabitants had been seen on several occasions.

"Yes, I saw the ghost about five years ago," stated one woman who worked in the building but understandably asked that her name be withheld. "He was standing in the mezzanine above me one evening when I was preparing to close up and go home. He was dressed in an old fashioned costume, and had a tall black hat. Because I was the only person supposed to be in the building at the time, he frightened me. Then I blinked, and he was gone! Just like that! This was my first and only experience with a ghost, and I hope my last! I know what I saw, and after that I refused to be in the building after dark, and never in the building at any time alone!"

Debi Cayer, Assistant Vice President and Branch Manager of Central Pacific Mortgage, who worked in the building from 1979 to July of 1981, and who brought this story to this reporter's attention, remembered these incidents. "The ghost in the building was felt by people working with me, loan officers, and other employees. People have certainly experienced the ghost and believe the building is haunted."

"I want to add that one evening, when I was alone upstairs, I heard strange banging sounds, as if someone was bumping and staggering into the furniture in the office that the *El Dorado Gazette* used to be in," another former employee told us. "When I called out, no one answered. I couldn't wait to get out of there!"

Placerville has a twisted and grim past. The ghost in the Chamber of Commerce building greatly resembles that of the official hangman of Hangtown. Many a hangin' took place on this spot.

No one knows if the Chamber of Commerce ghost is the hangman, or if the elevation of the mezzanine is the exact height of the scaffolds. The authors feel more investigation is needed and hopefully someone will take up the cause. After all, there is nothing sadder than a nameless ghost.

Placerville's Chamber of Commerce Building. Haunted by the town's official hangman, some say he is waiting for his next victim.

9

SUTTER CREEK
Sutter Creek Inn's Non-Paying Guests

Jane Way, a remarkable lady in all respects, found her life changed the day she purchased a 16-room New England mansion in Sutter Creek, with thoughts of making it a beautiful Inn. It seems the idea appealed to one of her non-paying guests. "I will protect your Inn," a spirit told her in 1966, and apparently he kept his word. The Sutter Creek Inn is one of the most lovely and enjoyable inns to visit in all the Mother Lode.

Traveling the winding, yet tranquil Highway 49 through Placerville approximately 32 miles, coming around a gentle hill, you will get a first glimpse of this well-kept town. Quaint, nestled in an instep of the High Sierras, the 1,200 foot elevated town is an artist's dream, a panoramic view of old, well-kept homes, and a boardwalk business area dotted with antique shops. Everything takes us back to the "olden days," probably not as it was, but as it should have been. Such is the way we found Sutter Creek.

The community was first named for John Sutter, our hero whose gold find triggered the gold rush. Sutter Creek, however, did not come into being until sometime around 1851, when a resident by the name of Leland Stanford was lucky enough to extract nearly one-half-million dollars in gold from a mine just outside the ramshackle town. Sutter Creek was to operate many mines during its day, including the last to operate in the Mother Lode, the Central Eureka, which closed its doors in 1959 after producing a whopping $25 million in gold.

The graceful white mansion, which is now Jane Way's Sutter Creek Inn, was first built in 1860 by John Keyes as a home for his beautiful young bride, Clara McIntyre. She was lonely for her native New Hampshire, and in his desire to please her, Keyes fashioned the home in the popular New England style. They lost their only child to diptheria when still a baby, leaving them only each other to love. Clara was devastated then, when Keyes died, leaving her a young widow at the age of thirty-four. Two years later the dashing State Senator Edward Convers Voorhies came to town and proceded to woo her. They were married on March 29, 1880, in her beautiful rose garden behind the house. The marriage produced two

The Sutter Creek Inn in Sutter Creek, haunted by a former state senator.

children, Earl, who died in World War II, and Gertrude who lived to be ninety.

"I bought the house from Gertrude just before she moved to a rest home," Way explained.

"It was strange," Way told the authors. "It was a rather unhappy time in my life. I purchased the Inn to get away from it all, and to make a complete change in my location and my life. I was, well, unsure."

"The evening the ghost appeared, I had been invited to a costume party. I was getting dressed, when an eerie feeling of being watched enveloped me. I turned around and there, standing in the doorway, was a tall man in old-fashioned clothing. For a moment I thought he was going to the same party, but I remembered all of our guests were gone for the evening. It was then that I heard the words, "I will protect your Inn." He managed to smile at me as he faded away. Well, I should have been frightened, but I felt warm all over. I knew then that I had made the right decision. Someone from outside my world was taking an interest in my affairs. What more could I ask for?"

"It was later that I saw a photograph of Senator Edward Voorhies. I recognized him immediately. I knew then that it was he who had visited me and said he was looking out for things."

Gertrude Voorhies, the former owner, also visits the house. "She lived in this place all her life and loved it dearly," Way was to tell us. "She told me often before she died how attached she was to the home. My experiences with the continuity of life was enhanced soon after Gertrude's earthly death. One evening she appeared in the parlor. She seemed to be checking things out, looking around. She apparently loved this house so much that she just could not stay away. She just had to come back!

"Another strange thing happened," Way told us, remembering. "My cat had just had kittens. She woke me in the middle of the night, and I suspected she was hungry. I got out of bed, put on my robe, and followed her to the kitchen door. As we approached the entry, she bolted and arched, refusing to go in. I looked into the kitchen but no one was there. I could not get her to go in. I was annoyed at her strange behavior, and I tried to coax her with little push, but she hissed and raised her claws at something unseen. I jumped back as in a flash, and without warning, her body was literally picked up out of thin air and flung cross the room.

"The poor cat seemed stunned and frustrated, as surely she was, and so was I. My heart was pounding! But soon after that the cat was willing to go into the kitchen as if nothing had happened and eat her food. I later learned that the original owner of the house hated cats!"

For all the ghosts, the Sutter Creek Inn remains one of the most popular resting spots in all of Northern California. Its rooms are booked well in advance, especially in the summer. "I guess that is because all of the ghosts are friendly," said Way. "At least to people."

"If you should see a ghost while you are here," Way advised us, "tell them they are welcome and to make themselves comfortable. They will make you feel that way!"

10

MOKELUMNE HILL
The Women Chasing Ghost of the Hotel Leger

The old-fashioned Hotel Leger in Mokelumne Hill is haunted by the original owner, an hysterical crying woman in the age-old theater, and a lady of disputable reputation in Room 7. In fact, the long dead floozy in that bedroom probably caused the demise of the innkeeper.

Quite untouched by time, Mokelumne Hill is a small community of approximately 1,500 people, nestled in the banana belt of the High Sierras. The elevation peaks at 1,450, and citrus grows all year around, contrary to surrounding areas which suffer extreme frosts and snow. An enchanted town, its inhabitants live in quaint old homes, most of which are colorful and well kept. Though the town is often besieged with tourists, it remains one of pride and a slowed country pace.

It was probably the climate that tempted George Leger, an immigrant from Hesse Castle, Germany, to settle in this gold-rush boomtown of 1851. From where he obtained his wealth we do not know, but he came into the area with enough clanging coin in his boots to establish a beer parlor on the site where he would soon develop his hotel, and enough cash left over to make a loan of $5,000 to a French Miller, the owner of a lumber company. The following year the Frenchman was unable to repay the loan, and Leger partially foreclosed on the lumber mill, conveniently making himself a senior partner in the company. In 1852 the beer garden was destroyed by fire, and with the lumber he now owned, Leger built a one-story hotel and called it the Hotel de L'Europe (The European Hotel). A second story was added to the building, and the first floor was converted into a general store. The second floor was used for room and board. A prominent dance floor made the hotel a very popular place to visit and entertain.

The Hotel de L'Europe was known throughout the country as one of the most luxurious in the Mother Lode. Old hotel ledgers bear the names of famous people from the world of government, arts and business. It was a popular meeting place for the elite.

But history repeats itself, and in 1879 a portion of the hotel was again destroyed by fire, and the illustrious owner upon rebuilding, renamed the establishment the Hotel Leger after himself. A civic-minded businessman, he served the community as chief engineer on the fire brigade, as Secretary to the French Benevolent Society, and ran a second business, The Sacramento International Insurance Association, out of the hotel. He seemed a pillar of society.

But Leger had one fault. He loved women. Too many women! And here begins the trail of clues with which to piece together the life, and afterlife, of George Leger.

On May 26, 1859, at the age of 43, Leger, a longtime bachelor married 25-year-old Louisa Wilkins. She died two years later after bearing him two children; a son, Albert Henry, and then a daughter, Matilda Rosina. A third daughter, Louisa, was born to George Leger, the birth certificate listing Louisa Wilkins Leger as her mother. The catch is, the document lists the child as being born one year AFTER the death of the mother! (This would be an amazing feat even with today's technology!)

As the authors see it, this can only be explained in one of two ways. An incorrigible womanizer, ol' George had an illegitimate child, and for the sake of convention had his dead wife's name admitted to the birth certificate as the mother. Perhaps he paid off the natural mother, and sent her on her way. He would then raise the child himself, no one the wiser except those closest to him. A proper member of society, one to be feared perhaps, no one would make gossip of this event, though it is interesting to note that years later, young Louisa's birth would always be celebrated as a year older than her chronological age.

The second explanation could also stand as truth in the gold-rush days. Perhaps his beloved Louisa indeed died in childbirth, as no records of the cause of her death are available. Perhaps the child she bore was to become her namesake, Louisa, in her memory. Records and recorders were often inaccurate in those days, facts being passed from hand to hand before they reached the county seat. Perhaps the wrong date had been pencilled in as to Louisa's death, or the year of the child's birth. Whatever the story, George was never to remarry, and verbally remembered Louisa as his one true love.

This did not stop him from enjoying the company of other women however! Not for a minute! The building next door to the hotel once housed a bar room downstairs, and a brothel upstairs, both of which were frequently visited by Leger before, during, and after his marriage. To this day the owners of the business which now inhabits these premises, The Lion and the Unicorn Catering, have seen and had amusing contacts with George and his eternal friends. They tell us he is anxious to continue frequenting these long-gone establishments.

But back to the beginning of his end.

George was a dashing figure of a man. Six foot tall, dark hair and moustache, he had piercing eyes that beckoned for adventure. He was forebodingly charming, and few women could resist his advances. This was unfortunately true of the girlfriend of W.H. Adams, Leger's friend, and the owner of the stage company which had the Wells Fargo contract between Stockton and Sacramento. As rumor has it, Adams' girlfriend, a high class but nonetheless brazen woman, took a fancy to Leger and often holed up in his hotel.

After a time, Adams tired of this competition for his woman's affections. He also owed Leger money and fretted about its repayment. His solution was callous. He hired a hit man to abruptly end the life of his former friend, thus ending all his problems.

As if to deliberately make Leger's last days on earth unbearable, Adams painstakingly hosted the man a final birthday party and invited (believe it or not) only MEN! For a man of Leger's appetite, this must have been the introductory offer to hell. A few months later, while coming out of Room 7 of his hotel, and the lustful arms of Adams' paramour, an unknown assassin shot Leger in the hallway.

Hearing the shot, friends and employees made their way up the stairs to the dying victim, ignoring the man with a gun dangling from his hand retreating in the opposite direction. The assassin reached the street unapprehended, and was never seen again. Leger's friends lifted his twisted body onto his bed, where he gasped his final breath. Adams was one of many at his side, sobbing.

No one knows if Adams and his girlfriend lived happily ever after, but years later, no one particularly the wiser about the crime, Adams was laid to rest beside the grave of Leger.

But all things must be forgiven in the after life, as Adams is often seen in the company of Leger these days as they haunt the Hotel and surrounding areas, chasing women, phantom and living, from room to room.

Ron Miller and his wife Joyce purchased the Hotel in June of 1987, and having heard the tales of the building being haunted from the previous owner, decided to go ahead with the transaction anyway. "What could a little ghost do?" Miller was to relate to us smiling. "Hell, I've been up against a lot worse than a few ghosts," he added. Not especially believing the stories the neighbors told, he went about his business of making plans for the hotel's restoration. As his wife continued to teach until the end of the school year in Southern California, he placed their children, aged 10 and 12, in school in Mokelumne Hill, and made a comfortable bedroom for them in the hotel.

Several days later the children came scrambling out of their bedroom. "Someone told us to be quiet!" they told their father. Upon investigation he could find no one. The children reluctantly went back to what they were doing. Later in the day they went into Room 7, which was during his life George Leger's bedroom. Seeing a picture of Leger on the wall, they told their father, "That man, the one in the picture, is the man who told us to quiet down." Miller looked at them quizzically.

Much to his surprise, a hired helper, Rel Rupe, confided in Miller that he heard noises in the hotel sounding like a banquet when the establishment was empty. He occupied the room above the old theater, and heard a woman crying. Rupe also doubled as a back-up cook, and told the authors he has on numerous occasions felt a ghost talking to him telepathically while finishing up his kitchen chores. "I believe George wants the place restored the way it was," Rupe told us. He also tells of an incident in the wine cellar. "George instilled in me the idea that the wine had not been stored properly and that I should go down there and check it out. I did, and sure enough, the wine would have gone bad if not attended to. George did us a good turn that time!"

On another occasion Rupe told us a waitress in the Hotel heard the sound of children. She insisted he go into the room and check. There was no one there.

Helen Alexander Woods, a pretty woman in her early 30's owns the adjoining business, the Lion and the Unicorn Catering Company. She and her husband Doug have been witness to several pranks and angry retaliations at the hands of George and his friends.

"The building I now occupy was a saloon, and the upstairs where we live, a brothel. We often see Leger and Adams at the house and business," she told us. "Last time, I guess I insulted them by changing some shelves around. They threw the cake pans off the shelf, and made a general all-around mess. During our remodeling they showed a real resistance to change," she remembered. "They moved things, and we could hear disgruntled voices not connected to any real (or alive) person. We finally decided to talk to them, letting them know that we were not in any way trying to exorcize them, and that we were only trying to improve the appearance of the building and make it more efficient. This seemed to stop them for a time, but they do come back on occasion just to look things over and be ornery. Every so often something will come up missing, and I will know George and Adams have been around again."

On Memorial Day, Miller was besieged with ghostly shenanigans as the hotel filled with guests. It apparently was a time George was in a rambunctious mood. "Several guests complained of a man chasing women down the hall late at night," Miller told us. "Some heard the commotion, others saw the escapades as they opened the doors to their rooms to see what was going on. But I do believe he was used as a scapegoat at one point," Miller said. "A window had been broken, and the guest said George broke it. The guest has been known to break things in a temper, so knowing the circumstances, I doubt if this was George's fault this time." Miller often has occurrences with George and his pal. "They make their way through the hotel, locking rooms from the inside, bumping into guests in the bar, and taking charge of events as they happen. "For instance," Miller said, "the simple task of hanging pictures can be an all-day job. If you don't hang something where George wants it, he simply throws the picture to the floor. I am learning to talk to him telepathically, listening to my inner voice, so as to avoid a few of these problems.

"Once I opened the door to George's bedroom and saw a shadow of a man stretched across it," Miller said. "Guests have also experienced this shadow in Room 7, and it is the least popular bedroom in the Hotel. Miller, who is known for always wearing a cowboy hat has had another strange and eerie circumstance happen to him on several occasions. "I am walking down the hall alone, when I see TWO shadows," he says. "One shadow is NOT wearing a cowboy hat!

"We have often wondered about the crying woman in the annex or theater," Miller stated. "She is not only crying, but wailing with a lack of emotional control. Guests have complained about this, as well as our neighbors. We wonder if it is Adams' girlfriend, sobbing at the loss of Leger, or another weary soul making its way through time here at our Hotel."

Whatever the circumstances, Leger at least is apparently more at ease now with the new owners. "A long missing 15 x 25 inch photo of Leger's children having tea was found hanging in the dining area one morning." Miller showed us the photo. "I guess he feels comfortable enough to have hung the picture of his loved ones," Miller said.

11

NEVADA CITY
The Mighty Ghosts of Nevada City

In March of 1850 a very important meeting was held in what was to become Nevada City. The year before, men were pulling a pound of gold a day from nearby Deer Creek. Regardless of the harsh winters, the hearty were determined to stay and find their fortunes. With this in mind, a name had to be found for the rapidly growing community of a thousand residents. After much deliberation, and a reminder of the terrible winter of the year before, the name Nevada was adopted, a Spanish word meaning "snow-covered." Thus settled, the menfolk again picked up pan and shovel to make their hopefully quick fortunes in gold. All was well.

It is unfortunate to note, fourteen years later, another residents' meeting was to take place on the same issue. It seems the state of Nevada had "stolen" this gold rush town's name when it was admitted into the union. Disgruntled, the townsfolk added a "city" to the end of their community's name so as not to be confused with the state of Nevada. Again the residents resumed the business of the day, the search for gold.

Throughout the 1850's and 1860's, Nevada City prospered and grew, despite seven fires of monstrous proportions that swept through the town as they did so many others in the gold-rush days. It seemed the word fire was synonymous with the era. Yet each time, in the spirit of comradeship, the citizens rebuilt. In 1860, Nevada City residents formed a volunteer fire department, a stand against destruction. As if to prove its might, in 1863, one of the worst conflagrations leveled most of the town. Eventually the town was rebuilt primarily in brick. In 1861, Nevada City erected not one, but two firehouses in an effort to avert fires. They were named, unimaginatively, Firehouse No. 1 and Firehouse No. 2.

According to a representative of the Searles Historical Library in Nevada City, "The residents of the town could not decide where to build the firehouse. The Main Street merchants wanted the firehouse down there, and the Broad Street merchants wanted to have it up there. They could never agree, and so they divided and each built their own. The wives of the Broad Street merchants went door to door and collected the needed funds faster than the Main Street Merchants, so though it was called Firehouse No. 2., the Broad Street Firehouse was constructed first, by about nine months." They were, and are to this day, as different in size and structure as could be possible. Firehouse No. 1 gave citizens reason to boast, as it was the finest, best equipped, and most beautiful of its day, a wooden and brick two-story structure, with Victorian bell tower and gingerbread trim added around the year 1866. Both served their purpose with updates until the year 1938, when a new, modern firehouse was constructed on Broad Street, a short distance from the former. Today Firehouse No. 2 is a warehouse. Firehouse No. 1 houses the Nevada City Historical Museum, and all the elusive ghosts therein.

Whether it was haunted in the days of its firehouse use or not, things certainly started to happen by the time the gold rush mementoes began to arrive.

A former director of the museum was to notice "cold areas and drafts in the building that were unaccountable." He heard footsteps when there was no one around. "I was alone, yet not alone," he was to say. The man tells of a Jesuit priest and two affiliates who toured the museum. When they reached the second floor, they turned to ask him who the red-haired woman in old-fashioned clothing was who sat down to play the antique piano the museum had inherited from an old whorehouse. As delicately as he possibly could, he explained the truth. "She is one of our ghosts," he said. No such red-haired person had ever been employed at the museum. Apparently, the redhead liked the piano when it was in the house of questionable repute, and decided to accompany it to its new residence. A former president of the Historical Society once unceremoniously shut a cabinet door which flew back open at her. It repeated this several times. Knowing about the many ghosts of the Nevada County Historical Museum, and being quite annoyed by this time, she told the unseen presence to "Stop this at once!" The cabinet door remained shut, but she heard footsteps walking away behind her. She was alone in the building. At least she thought so!

Many people have experienced ghosts upstairs at the old piano, the hutch, and the rocking chair. She appears to be the same brazen redhead, although there are reports on file of another spirit woman, this one in Victorian attire, rummaging through a cabinet, the doors of which are padlocked.

News of the haunted museum spread. On Wednesday, February 13, 1974, the *Sacramento Bee* front page headline read: "That Nudge in the Ribs in Nevada City House is Pushed Around by Exorcising S.F. Visitor." It tells of first-hand ghost sightings, of the feeling of being "pushed and shoved" while in the building, and a plea from Berg for a psychic to come to the building and exorcise the ghosts.

"It was the oriental ghosts that frightened me," stated Cheryl

Swope, speaking of her visit to the museum in 1987. The museum houses a thousand-year-old Taoist shrine from a joss (God) house in Grass Valley. It is believed to be the oldest in North America. Guests to the museum who stand before the shrine feel that they are being pushed, shoved, and tripped. "As I stood before the shrine, several figures of Chinese men materialized before me," Swope stated. "There were several of them, some kneeling, one walking around slowly, his head bent. I blinked a few times and they faded away. I heard a low, moaning sound, and my son heard what he described as chanting. We turned to leave, and my son tripped as if something had shoved him."

One of the most remarkable pieces in the museum is an 1880 photograph of an Irish miner by the name of Carrigan. The picture shows an ageing man with white hair and beard. To the side, and in the hutch, and in the same photograph, is the image of a young boy. As the story goes, Carrigan told the photographer that at the time of the sitting he was thinking about his childhood. He identified the youngster in the photograph as himself at about the age of twelve.

The firehouse museum is open 11:00 a.m. to 4:00 p.m., seven days a week. They ask a donation of 50 cents to defray costs. You might just get more than your money's worth.

Located at 107 West Main in Nevada City is the Hardscrabble Building. Constructed in either 1852 or 1856 (records differ), the building was designed for an undertaker who built his own caskets. The building of late was occupied by the Hardscrabble Antique Emporium, and the Hardscrabble Coin Store. Neither business remains in the building. Stories abound concerning the Hardscrabble building and its incarnate spirits. Perhaps some of the fleeting visitors from the building's mortuary days had stayed on to "greet their friends as the time came?" Who knows? At any rate, it could be fun speculating as you pass by.

Still, the most amazing ghosts of Nevada City, and the most illustrious, have resided at the Red Castle Inn through a succession of owners, remodelings, and occupants. They are, in a word, content and seem intent on staying through time immortal.

The most memorable of these ghosts seem to be the builder and original owner, and the "Lady in Grey," his children's governess who continues to serve.

Completed in 1860, the Red Castle Inn is a four story red brick edifice with elaborate gingerbread trim, constructed at the direction of its owner, John Williams, a former merchandiser from Illinois. The home was to be the fulfillment of a lifetime dream and promise to his beloved wife Abigail. Born of aristocratic stock Abigail knew the fineries of life. Making her his wife at the tender age of 15, Williams promised her, and himself, that he would somehow, some way, give her back the life she was accustomed to.

Nevada County Historical Museum, once a fire station, with all its ghosts and strange happenings. Some ghosts include the famed redheaded floozy from a long gone whorehouse, a more sedate looking woman in Victorian attire, and numerous Chinese ghosts, who trip guests who stay too long in front of their shrine.

They proved to be a loving family, devoted to one another. Abigail's only regret was her inability to produce a large family. She was only able to bear two children, a girl who died early in life, and a son, Loring Wallace. She loved children, and was to later take on a succession of foster children to raise and love.

But in the beginning years of their marriage, there was no time for thoughts like these! As the years passed, John tried many ways of endeavor to make money. Knowing of the gold rush and being preceded by Abigail's brother and his family to California, the golden itch seemed deserving of a scratching. To fulfill their dream, the senior Williams was eager to cash in on his share of the gold which was being found around Sutter's Mill. In his lead and always the adventurer, John, Abigail, and their now 17-year-old son Loring Wallace, set out for the gold fields of hopeful prosperity.

Life was hard, the distance tough. Mud and muck, dirt and sweat were okay for father and son, but not for his wife and mother. A decision was made to leave Abigail at her brother's home in Napa Valley, after which John and Loring Wallace continued their journey to the foothills. In 1850 they settled at Deer Creek Dry Diggins, which is an original name for Nevada City.

John sent a sketch of the home he hoped to build to Abigail. He described in detail the beautiful plot of land he had discovered and intended to buy when their fortune came in. By now fifty-five years old, it was this dream house, and his love of Abigail which stirred him to keep his aging body and emotional state together as he toiled the land in search of gold. In his mind he could not fail. It was his last chance for that promise.

Many hardships were to face the Williams men but despite setbacks, in 1860 John had enough gold to build his dream house on his own plot of land called, ironically, Prospect Hill. He was a happy man.

As Loring Wallace was by his father's side from the inception of the gold quest, he helped his father build and oversee the construction of the home. It would have approximately 4,000 sq. feet, which encompassed four floors, not including the brick framing and wrap-around verandah. The home would have sixteen rooms and a utility basement. There were to be two formal parlors, two master bedrooms, one for Abigail and John, the other for Loring Wallace and his new bride, a kitchen, entry and other rooms for the up to 11 children and foster children who, at different times through the years, would make their home at the Red Castle. Of these children (many orphaned by the hardships of the times), several had bedrooms on the third floor, the remaining having rooms on the 4th floor, along with the governess, for all time to be named the "Lady in Grey."

As predetermined, on the day of completion young Loring Wallace moved his family in along with his mother and father. The son had grown into an ambitious man, on his way to the top, with brains as well as stamina.

In 1855 he had taken Cornelia Elizabeth Humes, a woman of social grace, as his wife. He knew she would be an asset to his personal and career life, and their family swiftly expanded to four sons. During these years he obtained a degree as an attorney, and served as under-sheriff of Nevada City. In 1864 he started a successful law practice, and was appointed district attorney the same year.

For ten wonderful years John and Abigail enjoyed their mansion, their son and daughter-in-law, children, and friends within the community. They were respected members of society, and entertained lavishly in their beautiful home, a masterpiece even by today's standards. The parlors were to see many community events. Weddings for the elite were held around the unblemished terraced gardens. John was elected Justice of the Peace, and was called "Squire" by the townspeople. The dream had been fulfilled.

Unfortunately, as all things must come to an end, the inevitable did come to Squire John Williams on Wednesday, February 8, 1871, in his 68th year, in his dream residence, and in the arms of his Abigail. People talked of his bravery during his "painful, unknown illness" (probably cancer). His body was laid out as was the custom of the time in one of the ornate living rooms which had, in the past, seen joyous occasions. Friends came to pay their respects and offer assurance to the inconsolable Abigail. It was a dark time on Prospect Hill.

A long procession of wagons filled with friends accompanied John's body through the snow and bitter cold as he was laid to rest in the old cemetery. But apparently John's 'spirit' stayed home in the warm Red Castle.

After the funeral, things settled down primarily the same as when the Sr. Williams was alive, as Loring Wallace took over the family finances. Most of their holdings were in rentals and businesses. Having their buildings destroyed more than once by fire, and then rebuilt, their fortune was dwindling. Loring Wallace, inheriting these problems and being an acute businessman, tried to increase the family's holdings. The servants resumed their duties as usual.

For many years the family had secured the services of a live-in governess for the Williams' brood and foster children Abigail doted on. She was dowdy of dress, small in stature, dearly loved children, and was indeed, very good with those of this household. She took her job seriously, catering to the every whim and indiscretion of the younger residents, dealing each circumstance with her own brand of appropriate action. She was trusted by both Williams women and given a free hand with which to raise the children. Her name and background are unfortunately lost to us with time, but her indispensability and dedication were incomparable. She took great burdens off the family preceding the death of the senior John Williams, and for that they were eternally grateful. For refuge, she was given a small bedroom on the 4th floor of the Red Castle where she could shut herself off from the children when they were, at last, asleep for the night. Some say her only possession besides the clothes on her back was a little terrier dog which she often carried under her arm.

Three years later, on another stormy February day, a second death was to devastate the women of Red Castle as Loring Wallace passed through this life and into the next from his bedroom in the beautiful mansion. Being ill, and knowing the inevitable was near, he sold all his worldly goods to his wife for $1,000, with the exclusion of the home which was to remain his mother's. Eerily, as they had done all things together in life Loring Wallace's funeral would be held at the same time, and day of the week as his father's.

With the loss of the driving forces of their household, the widows were shaken with grief and worry. Neither knew the slightest about running a household, even less about the many businesses their husbands owned and oversaw. They feared they were edging slowly toward bankruptcy. One by one they relieved their servants of duties in an effort to save money, at last keeping only the governess for the remaining children. The grounds were to go to disrepair, the house a shambles.

Disaster after disaster!

Cornelia Elizabeth, frail since birth, died suddenly the morning of June 18, 1883, leaving Abigail to continue on by herself.

In 1891, feeble and old, Abigail knew she could not hold on much longer. The final indignity came when the once robust woman realized she could no longer rake the leaves and pine needles off the roof. She sold the home and adjoining lots for $1500 in gold coin. Abigail gave up her beloved Prospect Hill to eventually live in Southern California with one of her many foster children.

Rumor has it the unnamed governess was spared the trouble of relocating by an unexpected event. She was found dead in her sleep in her tiny bedroom shortly before Abigail was forced to move.

Of course the mansion was not known as the Red Castle in those days, and we know because so many years have passed that truths fall into "maybe" and "perhaps." But from here our story moves into other dimensions of reality, as the parties who witnessed the events are very much alive, and have given their testimonies as only they experienced them.

One such person is Jim Schaar, who purchased the run-down mansion in 1963, along with all the unnatural phenomena which is commonplace within the grounds and household.

"I grew up on the Monterey Peninsula amid all the beautiful old buildings and homes," Schaar said, "and I always had a dream of owning and restoring one. Seeing the Red Castle was the closest I have ever come to having a metaphysical experience. The moment I saw it, I knew I had to have it. I signed on the dotted line just hours after first laying eyes on

The Red Castle Inn, Nevada City
A gingerbread beauty, it hides some dark secrets and lusty ghosts.

it. Looking back, it seemed as if someone or something had taken hold of me. Later, when I returned home, I had a case of buyer's remorse. I truly had no idea how I would pay for it, but I just could not pick up the phone to cancel the deal."

Schaar's association with the Red Castle turned into a profitable one, as well as a learning experience of the nervous kind.

"I hired a handyman soon after moving in, and we went to work restoring the building. We started laughing about always looking over our shoulders, because we both had the unearthly feeling someone was watching us. When we looked around, there was no one there." Then, late one afternoon, the workman shed some light on the mystery. The specter materialized in front of him, showing concern about the work we were doing. He was able to describe the ghost in vivid detail, as the image remained fixed for some time. He later described it as "an old man ghost, in the attire of the 1800s...a black frock coat like a judge would wear...an old man doing a routine inspection, seeing how the work was coming along."

"I really didn't want to believe in ghosts," Schaar was to tell us. "I was afraid I might meet one face to face."

Jerry Ames owned the mansion from 1978 to 1986, and although he never saw a ghost through the years, he managed to keep his living guests and spirit residents happy if not, in all cases, segregated!

"Strange little things were always happening that we couldn't quite put our finger on," he was to explain. "For instance, my partner told me the Red Castle 'hid things.' He mentioned putting things somewhere and then could not find them. Later they would be found in another spot or part of the house.

"I think one of the strangest occurrences happened after a snow storm. There was a foot and a half of snow on the ground when a guest asked 'Who is the man on the deck? He's dressed rather strangely, in black and with a tall hat.' I knew of no guest that fit that description, and so we went to investigate. There was no one on the deck, and we were both startled to find no footprints leading to the deck. No mortal man could have been out there.

"Another time a guest asked me who was the oddly-dressed man crossing from one room to another room which was locked. At the time I knew the rooms were empty as the occupants had left to dine in town, it was reported the next morning. The guest swore he had seen a sober-faced person in a hooded robe."

One of the finest examples of materialization was to happen to an unsuspecting studious, middle-aged, male guest.

"The poor gentleman came into the doorway of the parlor," said Ames. "He was ashen. 'Who is David?' he asked, obviously shaken.

"We did not know what he was talking about. We checked our register and we had no one in the Inn by that name. As his story unfolded, we got our first glimpse of the children's governess, the Lady in Grey."

"I was asleep in bed when I was awoken by a pressure on my legs," the gentleman said. "As I got my bearing, I realized I couldn't move them because someone or something I could not see was sitting on them. As I struggled to push whatever it was off of me, out of the corner of my eye I saw a young woman standing in the room. She was dressed in grey, and seemed angry. 'David, DAVID!'[1] she said, as if to reprimand a disobedient child. The pressure on my legs lifted immediately, as if someone had gotten up, and she swiftly faded away."

During the years Jim Schaar owned the Inn, a very unusual experience was reported. "I had a New Year's Eve Victorian Dress Party," Schaar told us. "It was held for guests and townsfolk, and lasted well into the wee hours. Everyone was having a great time."

One woman, however, a non-drinker, had enough of the merry making and about midnight retired for the evening. As she settled into bed a woman came in, dressed for the occasion and carrying a small dog. She was dressed in a Victorian gown, and the guest remembered it being a soft grey color. She thought it odd her visitor should have a dog, for surely she

---

1. Due to lost records, it is unknown for a fact if any of the original children of the household was named David.

had not seen one at the party.

The Lady in Grey sat at the foot of the bed and patting the small dog, made pleasant conversation, talking about the party and other things of interest in a casual way to two people who had just met. After a while the woman stood and shifted the dog to her other arm. She smiled and said "Everything is going to be fine!" With that she left and closed the door.

The tired guest was a little puzzled about the last comment, but being so tired gave it little thought before falling asleep.

The next morning the guest looked for her new friend at breakfast. When she didn't see her, she inquired. The woman was told that all the guests who had been at the party were present. Besides which, no dog was or had been on the premises, to anyone's knowledge. She never saw her visiting friend again, but she had perfectly described the Lady in Grey.

We could not possibly list all the sightings of the Lady in Grey, nor the sightings of old John Williams. The grey lady has been seen in the Gold Room and hallways, also in the bedrooms, and most of all, on the top floor where she and the children resided.

And the new owners, Conley and Mary Louise Weaver, are not exempt from ghostly phenomena.

Mary Louise tells of a couple who went upstairs to the Grey Lady's bedroom to retire for the evening. A strange light appeared. There was not a light on in the mansion, and it was not a full moon. In fact, it was a very dark evening. There seemed no mortal reason for the light to be in the room. They felt an uneasy stillness as the unexplained illumination circled around the foot of the bed.

After blinking their eyes several times, and holding their breath, the light disappeared. Other less adventurous people might have wanted another room for the night.

During the same evening, Mary Louise was having her own light problems. She tells of going to a restroom which used to be a toy room off the children's bedroom, and finding the light on. She thought it strange as no one was around and the guests had retired for the evening. She checked her watch. It was about midnight. Shrugging her shoulders, she turned the light off.

The next morning while making her rounds, she noticed the light was back on. This time the door was closed. The room is directly below the bedroom where the guests experienced their mysterious light.

Employees of Mary Louise have had their moments with the ghosts of the Red Castle. One told of having a glimpse of a ghost in Civil War uniform with brass buttons in one of the children's bedrooms. A housekeeper, cleaning one of the bathrooms, looked outside into the hall to see the Lady in Grey drift by.

Recently the owners were startled to discover the balcony on the third floor locked. Under normal circumstances this would not be unusual, except this time it was locked from the outside. There are no stairs, no trellis, no way to exit the balcony from the outside.

It's lovely, it's enjoyable, it's enchanting to visit with the Weavers. Mary Louise is the perfect hostess, a combination of experience, charm and warm hospitality. She would probably be happy to tell you about the ghosts if you asked her, but then again, you might just see one for yourself.

12

DOWNIEVILLE
The Indelible Stain

Nestled in a basin walled by sheer, pine-covered mountainsides, Downieville lies at 3,000 feet across the upper Yuba River. The seat of Sierra County, it is a pleasant, picturesque community of less than a thousand residents. Once the population numbered in the thousands.

Today it has a museum exhibiting the objects that once enabled hardy men to wrest yellow wealth from its streams and mountains. The town's Methodist Church built in 1865, houses the oldest Protestant congregation holding continuous services in California. The gallows, last used for its grim purposes in 1885, is still on display, probably to remind that retribution is still a threat against crime. The *Mountain Messenger* is the oldest weekly newspaper in the state. For recreational use, the Greycroft Tavern once sported the longest bar in the Mother Lode country (70 feet). A stroll through the cemetery discloses interesting old epitaphs on graves dating back to 1850.

In November of the bustling year of 1849, Major William Downie arrived at the site with a motley band of followers. The group consisted of an Irishman, an Indian, ten Negro ex-sailors, and a gentleman of somewhat mysterious ancestry named Jim Crow. Happily, he never knew that his name would be identified with racial discrimination years later in America's Southland.

The major had noticed that the higher one went in the northern gold country, the larger became the nuggets. So he and his cohorts began climbing, despite grim warnings that winter had closed in. He was a man of great determination which approached foolhardiness.

Upon arrival to the area, the men found the river filmed with ice and a bitter wind blowing the snow into fleecy clouds. Downie had his men cut down small trees with their hatchets and erect crude cabins. Then he put them to work panning on the snow-covered river bars. It was cold, very cold, but they were encouraged by gravel rich with nuggets and yellow grains.

After only a few weeks, provisions began to run low, and decisions had to be made to avoid starvation. The major divided the recovered gold among nine of the miners and sent them to get food and supplies in the lower country. With one exception, all decided to continue looking for gold in a warmer climate and they vanished in the maelstrom of mining camps.

Only faithful Jim Crow came back in the spring, just in time to save Downie and three remaining miners from starvation. The major and his remaining companions quickly recovered, but now they had far too many competitors to share the wealth. Jim had been followed by a small army of gold-hungry prospectors who had heard the strikes were best in the Sierra foothills. Surrounding camps appeared on every bar and flat.

Downieville may well have been the richest region in the gold rush. At one camp the three owners filled their tin cups with gold dust every day. They named it Tin Cup Diggings. Once when Jim Crow had boiled a 14-pound salmon he found gold flakes on the bottom of the pot. In only eleven days four men took $12,000 worth from a claim 60 feet square. On Durgan's Flat, where the Sierra County Courthouse now stands, $80,000 in gold was found in the first half of 1850.

It must be remembered that outside the gold-rush region a dollar had such greater value that these amounts of money must be at least quadrupled to come even close to their real value. Outside the camp areas you could get a good hotel room for a dollar and a suite for two dollars. A loaf of bread cost a dime and a complete meal fifteen cents. At almost any saloon a nickel glass of beer would quench your thirst and sandwiches at the free-lunch counter would quell your hunger. Ah, the good old days!

It was a different story within the gold-rush country. Storekeepers, hotel owners and suppliers of mining tools charged exorbitant prices. A few miners attained wealth, but most left as poor as they had arrived. With hands that had never known toil and muscles that had never known pain, the merchants and dealers ended up with the gold.

In some of the hotels bread sold for a dollar a slice, and if you were in an extravagant mood you could get butter on your slice for another dollar. Eggs, when available, cost five dollars each. A potato set you back another dollar. We kid you not!

But the bed and the sandbars of the Yuba were wielding astonishing wealth. Though the normal was from 24 to 29 ounces a day, Downie and his companions were recovering 40 or more.

Near the Downie camp was a storekeeper named Bill Slater. In the midst of his shenanigans with his customers, he became seriously ill. Major Downie was a good-hearted man who lived by the Golden Rule. He took time off from his gold-seeking to nurse Slater back to health. Downie had formed a partnership with a fellow Scot, Jim Rose, who carried on the mining labor while Downie was occupied.

Slater recovered. And how he recovered! His wife, living in Sacramento, sent word to her husband that they were paying $22 an ounce there for gold instead of the standard $16. He offered to return the major's kindness by taking his gold to Sacramento and collecting the higher prices. Downie agreed, and gave him about $25,000 in gold plus an extra poke for his wife by way of appreciation. Word spread among the nearby camps and others gave Slater their gold to get in on this good deal.

After a round of handshakes, Slater took off to never be seen again in the diggings. Months later a man arriving at Downie's camp looked up the Major. "Met a man down in Panama with the name of Bill Slater," he said. "He was crossing the Isthmus with his new wife on his way to Europe. He said you were one of the best fellows in the world and always ready to help a stranger."

"So, that's what he said, did he!" Major Downie then voiced his opinion of Slater. We are forced to note that his statements are unprintable. They would scorch the paper, and we are attempting to write a book that could be read aloud at family gatherings without embarrassment.

Slowly the collection of camps became a town with permanent buildings, streets and a business district. Despite being seventy miles from the main source of supply, forty miles of which were dangerous mountain trails, the population grew to 5,000 in two years. Along narrow Main Street horses were tethered at night to posts holding up the wooden awnings. Boardwalks lighted by rays from kerosene lamps shining through windows were crowded by booted men.

In time there was a theater where the present movie house now stands. Here Edwin Booth, Lola Montez, Lottie Crabtree and other stars of the day entertained the show-hungry residents. They were rewarded with coins and gold pokes thrown onto the stage.

And there is the Costa Store. It was built in 1853 of uncemented shale with walls four-feet thick at the base and 27 scales still being used to weigh gold dust and nuggets. Gold still is occasionally mined around Downieville, but it is increasingly difficult to find and ever more difficult to extract.

A word about the ladies. God bless them. In the beginning there were no women in the camps. Then slowly some Mexican women drifted into the region as it became more permanent. The first Yankee woman to appear was Signora Elise Biscaccianti, a noted pianist of her day. She was welcomed by a large crowd of men whose cheers echoed and re-echoed from the steep-walled canyons of the Yuba. She was then carried on men's shoulders, as was her piano, to the finest quarters available.

There followed, of course, the camp followers of varied races. In the early days the scarcity of women was a hardship almost unendurable. The appearance of a woman brought miners from miles around just to look at her and follow her around. Women reminded the men of their faraway homes, of the families they had left behind.

As the camps became towns, brothels were established along with gambling houses and the ever-present saloons. But, as one writer states, "Generally speaking, the lowest of harlots was treated as respectfully as any pillar of the community."

At many of the camps there was more than one reason for this. They not only satisfied men's sexual needs, but many doubled as nurses. Sickness was frequent. The miners' diet of beans, sow-belly (salt pork) and saleratus bread, with occasional flapjacks, frequently caused scurvy. Only fruit, green vegetables and fresh meat, all rare in the region could have prevented these cases, although the strenuous physical labor of some healthy miners enabled them to escape the curse. So rare was fruit that one man paid a thousand dollars for a tiny plot with two apple trees.

So the stereotype of the prostitute with a kind, loving heart truly existed in the camps. They were friends. When they died crowds of grateful men attended the funerals and burials. Sometimes fences were erected around their graves. A few became legends in the annals of the West.

Only after 1855 when men began to bring their wives and lady friends to the camps and towns did the plague of scurvy start to end. The women planted gardens to raise green vegetables, and insisted that their men had proper diets.

But there is on Downieville's rich and colorful history a blot, a shadow, the unforgotten memory of one particular crime. For it was Downieville where the only woman during the gold-rush era was lynched.

Accounts of the short and tragic life of Juanita have been subject to distortion as it was told and retold through the years. Therefore we are indebted to William B. Secrest, author of the booklet *Juanita* (Saga-West Publishing Co, Fresno, CA. 1967).

He laboriously went back to the original and contemporary media and examined reports of what really happened. The reconstructed conversation in this chapter is based on eye-witness accounts and testimony recorded at the trial as ascertained by Secrest.

All accounts agree that Juanita was an attractive young Hispanic woman aged about 24. According to Major Downie, "She was of the Spanish-Mexican mixture, proud and self-possessed, her bearing graceful, almost majestic. She was, in the miners' parlance, 'well put up'." She was not a prostitute, but was living with her paramour, a slightly-built Mexican named Jose.

It was July 4, 1851. California had joined the Union the year before and this would be the town's first Fourth-of-July celebration. Thousands of miners came into town from the outlying camps. Flags were displayed everywhere. A platform had been built for the speakers of the day led by John D. Weller, later to be governor of California. There were bands and parades.

But it was booze that lubricated the occasion -- barrels of it that flowed like a mighty flood through the numerous saloons.

Lights and shadows punctuated the bizarre scene as thousands of miners staggered through the streets shouting and brawling. All afternoon the wild celebration continued. By late afternoon sober men were as scarce as fugitive criminals at a policemen's ball. The revelry went on into the night illuminated by whale-oil lamps.

There was probably no man more popular in the Downieville camps than Fred Cannon. He was a born leader, ruggedly handsome and chauvinistic. His impersonations were delightfully entertaining.

As the evening festivities continued, the miners collected into groups and held parties. At one such gathering, Cannon recited one of his most hilarious monologues -- a quarrel between a Chinese father, his daughter and her lover, imitating the voices of the characters.

It was past midnight when Cannon left the group. Leaving with Cannon were two friends, Charley Getzler and Ted Lawson. They proceeded to walk through the town on the board sidewalk singing ribald songs.

When they came to the front of Juanita's shack, Cannon fell against the door, ripping it from its leather hinges and throwing him onto the floor inside. Laughing, he picked up a scarf lying on the floor, scrambled to his feet and tied the scarf around his neck. Lawson later testified that he told Cannon to put it back.

Secrest writes: "What happened at this moment is a disputed point in California history. Some maintained that Cannon intentionally broke down the door with the idea of making advances to Josefa.[1] It was even asserted that he had been fruitlessly pursuing her for some time, but that she had spurned his attentions. Whatever the truth, it is definitely known that Josefa was in the room when Cannon tumbled in. Getzler's story was that he told Cannon to put the scarf back and that as soon as they saw Josefa, they put the door back in place and left. The drunken miners staggered off down the street and after a few ribald comments laughingly forgot the incident."[1]

Dawn heralded a new day destined to be the last in Juanita's short life. About mid-morning Cannon and Lawson appeared in front of the home and office of Dr. William Hunter which was located next door to Juanita's small shanty. Lawson testified later that they came to get some medication for Cannon. While they were talking to the doctor they were joined by Jose, Juanita's live-in lover.

---

1. Secrest uses the woman's Spanish name throughout his text, but has her anglicized name in his book's title.

"Senor Cannon," said Jose, "you busted my door down last night and you must pay me for it."

Cannon turned and regarded the small Mexican with annoyance. "I did not bust your door," he said. "Your door is so flimsy a passing dog could knock it down. Let's take a look at your damn door."

When the two men approached the door, Juanita came out, her features contorted with anger and speaking rapidly in Spanish. Cannon frowned. "Take it easy," he replied. "Why make such a fuss over a little thing like this."

Jose put his hand inside his coat. "Don't you dare pull a knife on me, Mex," Cannon said, "or I'll knock you down flat as a rug."

"No knife," Jose explained. "I won't fight you. You're too big and strong. Just pay me something for my broken door."

By this time a group of spectators had stopped and were listening to the argument. "I've got no more time to argue about this," Cannon insisted. "I got better things to do."

Still speaking excitedly in Spanish, Juanita moved between the two men. Jose seized her arm and tried to pull her toward the door. "That's right," Cannon said to Jose. "Take your whore inside and shut her up."

Jose managed to get her to the doorway. Cannon's remark now drove Juanita's already intense anger to a fever pitch. "I am not a whore," she shouted, her dark eyes flashing. "Don't you dare call me bad names. Come inside my house and call me that!"

At that instant Juanita was standing inside the doorway. Jose was behind her. Lawson was standing behind Cannon who was in front of the door. Cannon had no intention of allowing the spectators to see a pair of Mexicans win the argument and he was trying to calm her down. Juanita seized a knife from a table just inside the door and stepping forward plunged it into Cannon's chest. Cannon staggered back and fell into the arms of Lawson. His eyes widened with surprise as a crimson stain appeared on his shirt. "That bitch stabbed me," he half whispered as his knees buckled.

Juanita suddenly realized the gravity of her thoughtless, impulsive act. It was her fiery Latin temper that was to seal her grim fate. With a short scream she turned and fled to the Craycroft Saloon where Jose was employed as a card dealer. Jose followed her trailed by a number of witnesses.

Lawson and several friends carried Cannon to the doctor's office next door. Cannnon was growing weaker by the second., There was no hope. The knife blade had penetrated Cannon's heart. Lying on a couch, he drew his final breath and died.

At the saloon some of the startled gamblers tried to hide the woman. Her pursuers, however, were too close behind her. The enraged miners apprehended both Juanita and Jose. Meanwhile, news of the murder spread like a bush fire along the streets and through the camps. Crowds gathered in front of the doctor's office and the Craycroft Tavern. Juanita and Jose were taken to a log cabin on the side of the plaza near the speaker's platform. Cannon's body was taken to a large tent and placed on display. He was wearing a red flannel shirt unbuttoned to expose the wound on his chest. The exhibition only served to increase the anger of the visitors.

About two hours after the stabbing Juanita and Jose were marched to the speaker's platform where Senator Weller had orated the previous day. Around the platform an unruly mob of men pushed and shoved; many were drunk, others were nursing bad hangovers. Juanita strained her eyes, trying to see if there were any women among the spectators, but she was a tiny island in a sea of hostile masculinity.

At first there were shouts -- "Hang them now, let's get it over with." But one of the crowd's leaders climbed onto the platform and announced, "We'll give them a fair trial first, and then we'll hang them." It was a cry that was to become trite during the years of America's wild west.

A man named Jim Rose was appointed trial judge and twelve jurors chosen. William Spear was selected as prosecutor. Two lawyers, Pickett and Brocklebank, were appointed defense counsel.

Thayer, another attorney, mounted to the platform and protested against the informal trial with its mob atmosphere. But the crowd was not to be denied its kangaroo court and blood. It was in no mood for that kind of rational talk. He was pushed off the platform. According to George Barton, an eye witness, Thayer's feet never touched ground as he was beaten by the enraged miners for several hundred feet and finally left in a bruised heap at the far edge of the crowd.

Little wonder; David Barstow, another eye witness whose manuscript is in the Bancroft Library, Berkeley, Calif., wrote that the crowd of infuriated miners were "the hungriest, craziest, wildest mob standing around that I ever saw anywhere." (He failed to tell us how many mobs he had ever observed.)

The first witness was a boy named Frank, aged about twelve. He promised Judge Rose he would only tell the truth. He testified that he was present at the time of the stabbing, and that the woman seemed very angry and determined.

He was followed by Dr. Hunter. He said he had not observed the incident, but that he had known the deceased very well and found him to be a "remarkably athletic but peaceful man."

Ted Lawson was next. It was his account of the actions preceding the stabbing that we have presented. He insisted that Cannon had remained calm and collected while Juanita had displayed "a great deal of temper and determination."

Charles Getzler described the part of the previous night, how the door was broken down by Cannon's fall, and the picking up and returning of the scarf.

At this point, Judge Rose instructed a man named McDonald, a carpenter, to go to the prisoners' cabin and examine the door. Upon his return he stated that the door was very frail and he could find no hinges on it.

The testimony of a Mr. Knowles agreed with that of the boy Frank and Lawson. As a partner of Cannon, he had come looking for his friend and found him in front of Juanita's house engaged in an argument. He too, said Cannon had not lost his temper, but most definitely Juanita had.

Next came Richard Martin. He testified that he lived in a room adjoining that of the prisoners. The wall between was not very thick. Right after the door-breaking incident, he had overheard the conversation between Juanita and Jose. Although the talk was in Spanish, he understood some parts of it.

Present at the trial was a reporter for the *Pacific Star*, a Marysville newspaper, who had been sent to cover Senator Weller's speech. He wrote: "Here the witness explained what the conversation was, which it is unnecessary to repeat as it was obscene. He knew the meaning of the language used, he said, from having been informed by the prisoner, Jose. On this explanation in broad language, the prisoners seemed highly delighted and laughed heartily."

This closed the case for the prosecution. Attorney Pickett now requested the court to permit the prisoners to make statements in their own defense. Permission was granted. Jose, described by the *Star* reporter as "a quiet, inoffensive sort of man," stepped forward. His account was identical to those of the previous witnesses. He added, however, that Cannon had called Juanita a whore, and then he had tried to enter the house while still calling her bad names. That was when she had been forced to stab him.

Now it was Juanita's turn. "First," asked Judge Rose, "how well did you know the deceased?"

"Only slightly," she replied. "He wanted me to have sex with him once. I said no, that I had my man." She glanced at Jose.

"You may proceed," said the Judge.

Juanita related the events leading up to the stabbing, then she added: "I took the knife to defend myself. I had been told that some of the boys wanted to get into my room and sleep with me; a young Mexican boy told me so. It frightened me so that I used to fasten the door and take a knife with me to bed. I told the deceased that was no place to call me bad names, to come in and call me so and as he was coming in I stabbed him."

Judge Rose then adjourned the trial until one-thirty to permit the defense to prepare its case. As for Colonel Weller, David Barstow, an eyewitness, stated that Weller was seated on the platform during the trial but remained silent. On the other hand, Hubert H. Bancroft, the noted California historian, in his book *Popular Tribunals* (San Francisco, 1890) writes that Weller refused to even attend the trial or to intervene on behalf of Juanita. If we may pause to be cynical for a moment, how can we weigh the fate of a voiceless Mexican woman against thousands of potential voters.

When the trial resumed, the first witness was a Mr. McMurray. His testimony was that he saw Cannon stagger, but he didn't see the actual stabbing. He added that he had heard Cannon call the woman a whore.

The final witness was Dr. Cyrus D. Aiken and he dropped a bomb. He said that Juanita was about three-months pregnant and if she was hanged two lives would be taken. The court, he added, would do well to consider this before acting rashly.

This angered the lynch-mad mob. Were they to be denied their thirst for blood? Was this a trick to thwart justice? There were cries of "hang her now" and "hang the Doc with her." Hostile miners pushed forward and threatened to rush the platform.

Judge Rose raised his arms. "We will get proof if this is so," he shouted. He quickly met with the counselors and jury and all agreed that the opinion of other physicians should be sought. The judge appointed Drs. Hunter, Hardy and Chamberlin to retire to a nearby shack and examine Juanita.

A few minutes later the doctors returned. They announced that they did not agree with Dr. Aiken. They had found no evidence of pregnancy. The crowd roared its approval.[2]

There was no more testimony. Judge Rose retired the jury. Fifteen minutes they were back with their verdict:

"The jury finds that the woman, Juanita, is guilty of the murder of Frederick Cannon, and that she suffer death in two hours. The man Jose is found not guilty, but the jury earnestly request that Judge Rose advise him to leave the town within twenty-four hours. Amos L. Brown, Foreman."

There was no hysteria, no weeping, not even a frown on Juanita's part. As she was led away by several appointed guards, she remained stony-faced. She was taken to the nearby cabin where she had earlier awaited her trial. There she was allowed to see any of her friends she chose and to pray and make her peace with God.

Jose came to bid her good-by. It was the one time throughout Juanita's ordeal that she could no longer conceal her emotions. As they hugged and kissed for the last time, tears rolled down her cheeks. "You

---

2. Years later the widow of Dr. Aiken told Mrs. Fremont Older, author of *Love Stories of Old California*, that her husband had lied in an attempt to avert the tragedy.

must go," she finally whispered. "Go quickly and please don't look back."

Judge Rose appeared at the door. "I'm sorry lady," he said. "The time has come." With two guards at her sides holding her arms, Juanita began her final walk. It was a perfect July afternoon. A gentle breeze was blowing down the canyon from the mountains. The sky was blue with fleecy-white clouds in the distance. Juanita was taking her last look at the world she was so soon to leave. It was four-thirty.

They came to the Jersey Bridge, a wooden structure that spanned the Yuba. Down below the river flowed in its ceaseless journey to the lowlands. Overhead a warm sun was still high in the western sky. Here the makeshift gallows was waiting.

The scaffold consisted of a wide plank held four feet above the bridge floor by ropes at each end. The ropes passed over and under the railings on each side and then up to the super structure where they were tied. The rope with the noose was also tied to the super structure. When the signal was given, two men would simultaneously cut the plank ropes at each railing, thus dropping the plank out from under the prisoner.

Again we turn to the account written by the *Pacific Star* newspaper reporter: "At the time appointed for the execution, the prisoner was taken to the gallows, which she approached without the least trepidation. She said, while standing by the gallows, so I was informed, that she had killed the man Cannon, and expected to suffer for it; that the only request she had to make was, that after she had suffered, her body should be given to her friends, in order that she might be decently interred.

"This request was promptly complied with (and) she extended her hand to each of the bystanders immediately around her, and bidding each an 'adios senor,' voluntarily ascended the scaffold, took the rope and adjusted it around her neck with her own hand, releasing her luxuriant black hair from beneath it so that it should flow free.

"Her arms were then pinioned, to which she strongly objected, her clothes tied down, the cap adjusted over her face, and in a moment more the cords which supported the scaffolding had been cut, and she hung suspended between the heavens and the earth."

There was a spasmodic jerking and twitching as her lungs fought for air. It ended in a final convulsion as she swung her bound legs back and forth, then came the blessing of black unconsciousness.

There are some events that are always remembered: The first day of school, the loss of virginity, graduation, an operation, a marriage. And there is another: witnessing the deliberate execution of a fellow human being.

As the gravity of what they had just observed was realized by the spectators, a blanket of silence fell over them. One by one as individuals, and then in groups, they drifted away, back to the saloons where they would try to drown their memories in alcohol. Behind them they left the

The bridge constructed on the exact spot where Juanita, the woman with the distinction of being the only woman hung during the gold rush days, met her final breath.

body of a small woman slowly turning in the early evening breeze. Sometime during the night several now compassionate men cut down Juanita's body and carried it to the home of one of her friends.

The appointed grave diggers were anxious to get back to their more profitable diggings -- for gold. It takes less time to dig one large grave than two separate ones. So the bodies of Juanita and Cannon, the slayer and the slain, were laid side by side in one wide grave in the Downieville cemetery. There in the democracy of death, their conflict faded into oblivion.

There is a final grim chapter in the story of Juanita. It was the ultimate insult to the memory of a short-tempered, but very brave and victimized woman.

A few miles east of Downieville is Sierra City, another gold-rush town by the North Fork of the Yuba River. It was here at the Monumental Mine that a 100 pound gold nugget was found in 1860. Here, too, is the imposing Busch Building built in 1871, its first two stories of brick with a third story and balcony of wood. Above one of the doorways are the initials "E.C.V.," standing for "E. Clampus Vitus," a fraternal organization that happily exists today only in history books.

The lodge originated in Pennsylvania in 1847 as a hoax, a parody, a satirical travesty of Masonic orders and other serious fraternal societies being organized at the time. Its rituals were secrets known only to members. This "Incomparable Confraternity," as it came to be known, spread across the country, reaching the Mother Lode region in about 1852.

Within a few years every mining community of any size had its chapter. The mysterious brotherhood became so powerful that newcomers found they could not conduct business until they had joined it. When Lord Sholto Douglas came to Marysville with his theatrical troupe, he found the first night audience too small to pay for the rent of the theater. Enlightened by a friendly miner, he applied for membership. Thereafter the miners flocked to his company's presentations.

Described as "masterpieces of ingenious and humorous torture," the initiations allowed members to inflict their sadistic desires on initiates. Only those who survived them understood what E.C.V. stood for.

Sometime in the 1870's the Downieville cemetery was moved to a new location to permit the site to be searched for gold. George Barton, the local historian, writes that at that time Juanita's skull was stolen and for some years thereafter it was used in the initiation ceremonies of the local E.C.V. chapter. Although this particular ceremony is not on record, we know how skulls have been used in similar secret societies. The initiates have been instructed to drink an alcoholic beverage from the skull. What happened to the skull after the Downieville chapter disbanded will never be known. Like the skull of a noted Indian Chief, it may have ended up as an ash tray.

The wooden bridge upon which Juanita died was washed away in a flood years ago. Today at the site a modern steel bridge spans the Yuba. At one end of the bridge is a building and on this structure is a plaque. It reads: IN MEMORY OF JUANITA, THE SPANISH WOMAN, LYNCHED BY MOB FROM ORIGINAL BRIDGE ON THIS SITE JULY 5, 1851. Downieville remembers!

But the tragedy has a quite different legacy -- the apparition of Juanita, which psychically sensitive residents and visitors have observed on or near the bridge. Such a person is Mary Hansford, a former Downieville resident. This is her account:

"I once worked in one of the stores in this community," she told us. "As I became acquainted, many people told of seeing the ghostly Juanita, but I thought they were just superstitious. After all, this is a small town with very close people. I figured it was a story passed on from one generation to another to scare the children. I was quite startled a few months ago when my car broke down. I decided to walk home because it was such a beautiful clear night.

"When I came to the Downieville bridge, I saw what appeared to be fog in one corner. As I approached, I saw the face of Juanita. She was dressed as one would be long ago. She was silently uttering words, trying to tell me something.

"I was frightened and backed away, but I guess I didn't have to. She seemed no longer aware of my presence. She looked up, closed her eyes, and disappeared. Just like that! I can positively affirm that I saw her. I am no longer a skeptic."

James Kellog, a longtime resident, is another witness. "When I was a lad I could expect to see her every now and then, and I still do. We can do nothing for her, but most townsfolk have learned to take her in their stride. I hope someday she will find peace."

Parapsychologists tell us that hauntings can be caused by extreme emotional energy experienced by people long gone. Therefore, they hypothesize, certain locales have built up their own "atmospheres" over the years. These auras can be felt by sensitive persons who encounter these remnants caught in the web of time.

13

WHAT IS A GHOST?

We are pleased to call the physical world around us the final reality. But there are as many realities as there are means of perception. The reality of one may be the illusion of another. And adjoining this reality borders one perceived by humankind from time immemorial.

As Mark Twain once wrote, this border realm may be the "real world" while we dwell in physical life in the "shadow world." In this strange realm are the seats of mind, consciousness and life itself. This physical body may be a shell and the chemical cellular brain the tool of the mind.

What, then, are ghosts?

There are many different kinds of apparitions that manifest in this borderland between worlds or dimensions. In addition to humans, there are specters of animals, domestic and wild, like the black dogs of Britain and the New Jersey devils, appearing and disappearing within the limited ranges of our senses. The annals of parapsychology contain many accounts of buildings that briefly exist along haunted roads.

There are the ghosts of earth's seas, vessels that come with eerie phosphorescence from out of the vast deep, observed by experienced and reputable seamen and duly recorded in the logs of civilian and military ships.

And there are the islands, drifting in and retreating from the mists of the great unknown. Landlubbers are astonished when they first see numerous islands marked on nautical charts with the initials E.D. (existence doubtful). Among these mirages of mystery is Dougherty, its position established by nine mariners. Then it vanished. There are the Auroras, immortalized by Edgar Allen Poe in his story "Arthur Gordon Pym." Today no vessel can find them.

In the atmospheric sea above us are unidentified flying objects (UFOs). Seeming at times as unsubstantial as clouds and at other times as solid as aircraft, they comprise one of our century's most uncanny mysteries. What are they? Where do they come from?

But it is the phantasms of humans that interest us at present. There is no simple explanation of these appearances. The parapsychological evidence is that they have a number of origins that we will now consider.

EARTHBOUND ENTITIES

The usual concept of a ghost is a departed spirit dwelling in a building it presumably knew in physical life. Such a belief implies that an individual, perhaps after an unhappy wretched life, is condemned to endlessly and for no apparent reason haunt a place, continuing the appearance and even the clothing it once possessed. Can this be a fate decreed by a omniscient and benevolent providence? We shall see, however, that there are more reasonable explanations for these passive apparitions.

But it seems there are occasional earthbound spirits.

The late Eileen J. Garrett was no frail secluded medium or psychic sensitive. She was a lively, level-headed business woman who launched a New York publishing concern, originated and edited *Tomorrow* magazine, had an Irish sense of humor and a healthy skepticism about some aspects of her own abilities. *Life* magazine called her "the best known and reliable psychic in the world."

In her autobiography *Adventures in the Supernormal,* she wrote:

"Normal death is not an instantaneous event, but a process that in some cases involves a long time before life is finally and completely released. I have known of cases in which there has been evidence of a partial "consciousness" remaining in ghostly form for years after the death of the body, as though some part of the mind were reluctant to release itself. So far as my own experience, the lingering here is due to some injustice, injury or moral wrong which the consciousness has not been able to forgive or forget, and which under the mysterious law of compensation, arrests its progress and holds it in the place of its deepest life relationship."

A survey of such cases in psychic records reveals the following reasons for earthbound conditions: To change or locate a will, desire for a proper burial, help for a sick or otherwise endangered relative or friend, to prevent a material misfortune, to bring a murderer to justice, to save one's good name, and to help in an emotional crisis.

Such cases, however, are rare. As Eileen Garrett writes: "It would seem to be that out of the millions that are dying all the time, relatively few are caught and kept in mid-space...It is well that such lives are not more numerous -- at levels that are perceptible to us, at least."

ETHERIC FORMS

Chief Engineer Harold Eastman, of the Rhodes Electrical Society in London, was working on some high-tension wires in a dark room when he saw a luminous blue sphere form about a revolving dynamo. In the center of this sphere a woman's hand suddenly appeared. Eastman asked his assistant, a Mr. Woodew, if he could see it, and he replied that he could. Both men watched the phenomenon, and they were able to ascertain every detail of the conditions causing it.

The two men spent four days trying to produce the occurrence again, and when they succeeded a human head, instead of a hand, appeared. Photographs were taken and they were published in several European journals in the summer of 1930.

A follow-up to the Rhodes observation was an article printed in the *Revue Spirite* (Paris), written by M. Henri Azam. M. Azam has obtained his material from an experimenter who desired to remain unknown except to the publication's editors. This unknown student was quoted as follows:

"In the pursuit of my specialized work in the occult and psychic fields I long desired to find out whether it was possible to reconstitute the astral form by means of sound vibrations. It was my belief that mediumistic phenomena, when they are serious in character, are exclusively the result of setting in action some force for which the medium is the condenser. It was my purpose, therefore, to reconstitute a sphere of synchronous vibrations analogous to those which emanate from the human entity, but to do so without the intervention of any medium..."

The following methods were used by the experimenter. Two machines of static electricity were arranged so that the plates would turn in opposite directions. The positions and distance between the plates were so arranged as to be susceptible to infinite variation. As a result there was a variable and sensitive magnetic field formed. A membrane covered with lycopodium powder was placed at the variable point so that it vibrated according to the electric wave lengths employed. The vibrations were intensified by adding the factors of light, sound, and perfumes. A magic lantern was directed upon the variable point for light effects; an organ was used for sound effects.

"Under these conditions on several different occasions I was able to obtain the formation of human and animal forms, which appeared in the magnetic field. At first these were only partial, but twice I succeeded in obtaining complete forms. They always presented themselves in the sensitive field and near the variable point. Three photographic negatives, exceedingly clear and sharply defined, were obtained of these vibrational forms."

The conclusions of the experimenter are that he has been able to obtain responding vibrations of the astral or psychic world; that the results cannot be ascribed to imagination or hallucination; that the forms which appear are not spirits, but empty and discarded etheric or astral bodies or shells; that it is therefore possible to obtain psychic phenomena without the aid of human mediums.

Man, both in physical and psychic terms, is an exceedingly complex being. The astral body is an exact replica of the physical body, which it interpenetrates, but is composed of finer matter. It is the "spiritual body" of St. Paul, and has been given other names in various cultures. Etheric bodies, according to the theory, are considered links between the physical and astral bodies. They are abandoned soon after physical death and they slowly disintegrate in a vibratory plane known as the "astral cemetery" which lies very close to the vibratory limits of our visible physical plane.

It is also supposed that these empty etheric shells remain close to the decaying physical bodies until they are dissolved into their original basic elements. Being held nearby by various subtle affinities, these etheric shells are said to be the cause of reported graveyard phantoms. Abandoned by progressing astral bodies, these apparitions seldom display evidence of animation.

A friend of the writer, a state patrolman, once told of seeing a number of phantoms during a severe electrical storm when he was caught in a local cemetery. They were simply white human-like forms hovering above the graves glimpsed during flashes of lightning. Many similar accounts can be found in psychic annals, along with battlefield apparitions of an etheric type.

THOUGHT FORMS

Some ghosts may be creations of human consciousness. The late Carl G. Jung, the noted Swiss psychologist, postulated that just as we as individuals possess unconscious minds, there may exist a universal unconscious, a reservoir of mass human thought. The mental creations that existed in this pool of thought and belief he called archetypes. These archetypes could emerge and manifest under certain conditions.

This may explain the appearances of ancestral and traditional ghosts. Called forth by the imminence of a death we have the Irish Banshee, the White Lady of Berlin, and the Phantom Nun of Yorkshire, England. If enough individuals believe that a specter haunts a certain location, is it possible that their united belief may create a manifestation?

A group associated with the New Horizons Research Foundation, Toronto, Canada, decided to see if they could create a ghost. They met weekly to invent a detailed history of an entity including his birth, where he had lived and various aspects and incidents in his life. They named him "Phillip."

When he became real enough in the minds of the group, they tried to communicate with him. Although Phillip never became visible, at the end of a year he was tilting tables, producing raps, and offering information and advice.

In the ancient East psychic processes are far better understood than here in the West. In the Orient adepts for millenniums have sought knowledge within themselves and their minds, while in the West the search has been external and technical. One of the more rare abilities of advanced adepts is to use prescribed meditation and visualizing exercises to materialize a human apparition or thought form.

In Tibet the practice is known as dubthab and the apparition is called a *tulpa*. Alexandra David-Neel, the noted French world traveler and occultist, tells of her experience in her book *Magic and Mystery in Tibet*. She succeeded in creating a monk-like figure who was certainly no subjective illusion since it was observed on many occasions by others.

David-Neel tells us that she had chosen a character short, fat and jolly for her mind-creature. After a few months the *tulpa* gradually underwent a change. His body became leaner. His face assumed a mocking, sly, malignant look. He became bold and troublesome. She had lost control of her mental Frankenstein.

She wrote that the phantom's presence became a "day-nightmare." Deciding to dissolve the *tulpa*, it required a reversal of the process during six months of exhausting struggle. The mind-creature was tenacious of life.

A distinction must be made between creation of a *tulpa* double by an adept and the projection of one's astral body. Dr. W.Y. Evans-Wentz, in his *Life of Milarepa*, says that the great sage projected a number of *tulpas* of himself while dying. Many of his followers in places far apart thought they had encountered Milarepa himself.

Bilocation, or being seen in two (or more) places at the same time, is an ability attributed to many saints and mystics throughout the centuries. One of the latest is Padre Pio, the famed stigmatic Italian monk. His visitations for healing as reported in *Mysteries of the Unexplained* (Reader's Digest, 1982) were probably astral projections during meditation.

AKASHIC IMAGES

From the ancient East, too, comes the concept of the Sanskrit Akashic Records. This is the belief that every scene, every event, that has taken place at any particular point on the surface of the earth has been permanently registered in the "ethers" surrounding our planet. In western terms this reservoir of images is also known as the Earth Memory.

It is this realm that enables the clairvoyant and the psychometrist to obtain supernormal knowledge. Then, too, in certain locations the barrier between the physical and the Akashic may become thin. There are quite a number of cases in psychic annals of buildings, lakes, roads and streets appearing and disappearing. Sometimes such illusions can be disturbing and frustrating.

Janet Bord, the British writer, tells of a cottage in a wood near Haytor, Devon, that has been observed by various witnesses over the years. Neighbors living nearby report that it comes and goes regardless of external conditions. Once a Ordnance Surveyor checking the area looked down from a high vantage point and saw the cottage he had missed before. He walked down to the spot but all he found were grass and trees.

John Swain and his family have been searching for a phantom lake near Beaulieu Abbey in Hampshire's New Forest. "We were driving down some little, off-beat lane seventeen years ago when we saw the lake. Then we saw a boulder with a sword sticking out of it about fifty yards from the shore. We thought it was some sort of memorial to King Arthur. We were all fascinated by the scene." About once every three weeks the Swains drive a hundred miles to search for the mist-shrouded lake. It cannot be found. There are many similar tales.

Thoughts are things. They do not simply vanish. Thought activity extends beyond the physical brain as is evident in telepathy and the collective unconscious. Thoughts, actions and feelings are somehow impressed or encoded into a field of mind energy that seems to surround the earth.

It is one of the discoveries of modern science that all things possessing life are composed of energy patterns. At times of acute emotion we humans seethe with chemical and electrical activity. Such concentrations of energy are apparently encoded into the atmosphere or ethers at the scene of the disturbance. In some haunted houses the sensitive witness sees a re-enactment of a murder, suicide or similar emotional event. It is the scene itself that is the haunting, not the psyches of the performers.

Margaret Murray, the noted anthropologist, in her autobiography *My First Hundred Years,* suggested that ghosts are a form of photograph. She pointed out that apparitions are usually seen in houses or sheltered places and wearing the same clothes in which they were last seen.

Dr. Murray writes: "This seems to me strongly suggestive of a photograph, a writing caused by light on some combination of the constituents of the air... It should be remembered that in photography though the light waves are recorded on a prepared surface, the result is not visible till the surface is specially treated, otherwise the surface...remains blank. I suggest that it is also the case with apparitions."

Many parapsychologists, such as W.G. Roll of the Institute of Parapsychology, support the theory that objects can be impregnated with a person's psychic energy. Occasionally, instead of a visual image, such energy traces or impressions can be auditory. They may manifest as voices, footsteps or thumping sounds.

GHOSTS OF THE LIVING
The belief that man is composed of two counterparts, a physical body and a psychic body, the latter being the vehicle of the mind and consciousness, has been universally accepted for centuries. This second body of tenuous composition normally coincides with the physical body. It has been given many names, the better known being the astral, psychic,

mental, and more recently the parasomatic body. It is a duplicate of the physical body and is complete, that is, if a physical limb is lost the astral limb remains, which may be the real explanation of the "phantom limbs" experienced by amputees.

The astral body can leave the still-living physical body and return to it. The projected body is at all times in communication with its earthly counterpart by means of a line-of-force, a sort of elastic cord akin to the umbilical cord of physical birth, across which flows an energy maintaining life in the unconscious body. This cord is capable of infinite expansion.

There are involuntary projections that may, or may not, be consciously experienced. They can be caused by anesthetics, shock, certain drugs, extreme illness, accidents, hypnosis, and suppressed desires. There are also voluntary self-projections brought about by certain exercises and mental practices. Both types are now known as "out-of-body experiences" or OBEs.

OBEs have been reported by persons in all walks of life. Novelist Ernest Hemingway experienced his projection during World War I when a mortar shell exploded and he suffered leg injuries. Others who have written of their experiences include C.G. Jung, the Swiss psychologist; Cromwell Varley, the inventor; Cora L.V. Richmond, the peace advocate; Caroline D. Larsen and Gail Hamilton, short story writers; William Seabrook, the travel author; and Sax Rohmer and William Gerhardi, British writers.

Pioneered by Dr. Elizabeth Kubler-Ross, a number of doctors in recent years have collected and studied OBEs of patients who have undergone clinical death but have been revived. All of these cases regardless of culture, East and West, have followed a pattern that seems to eliminate hallucination. They attain consciousness while floating over their physical bodies, observe what the doctors and nurses are doing which is later confirmed, pass through a tunnel which has a light at the end where they meet a "shining being." At this point some patients may be told that they must return to physical life as their time to die is yet to come. This would indicate that at least for some of us a time to die is foreordained.

Dr. Kenneth Ring, of the University of Connecticut, was the first to scientifically document the fact that people who have OBEs at the point of death show a marked reduction of death anxiety. After a survey, Dr. John Palmer, of the University of Virginia, in an article in the *Osteopathic Physician* (April, 1974), states that "Many people who have had striking OBEs report that the experience convinced them of survival after death and eliminated their fear of death." As with others who have successfully projected their astral bodies, this writer shares this view.

Research in this phenomenon has been conducted in an increasing number of universities and prestigious laboratories. Persons who can project at will have been studied by Dr. Charles Tart, University of

California at Davis; Drs. Stuart Twemlow and Fowler Jones, Topeka V.A. Hospital; Stanford Research Institute, Menlo Park, Cal.; Institute for Parapsychology, Durham, N.C.; Mundelein College, Chicago, Ill.; and the Lawrence-Berkeley Laboratories in northern California.

The projected astral bodies, either spontaneous or experimental, have been observed by other persons as apparitions in normal environments. There are quite a number of such incidents in psychic annals. Therefore the "ghost" you may happen to see could be the projected astral body of a still-living person.

If we could fully understand all the relationships between time and space, most of the mysteries in psychic phenomena would be solved. This will never happen in the foreseeable future. Each discovery and theory raises more questions than they solve. J.B.S. Haldane, the great British scientist once wrote: "The universe is not only stranger than we imagine; it is stranger than we can imagine." He was referring to this fundamental problem.

Our linear concept of time is deceptive. An effect does not always immediately follow a cause. This is evident in premonitions and prophecy. It is evident in the two-way time theory of Dr. Gilbert Lewis, of the University of California, who suggests that time moves in two directions -- backward and forward. This means that there is no positive future or past, but that one exerts a "pull" on the other. Events of today may have been a cause of certain events in history. The law of cause and effect is disturbed when various events are destined to happen.

This brings us to synchronicity. Here we have two events, perhaps separated by time and space, coming together to form a meaningful coincidence. A farmer's wife loses her wedding ring in a potato field. Forty years later she finds her ring inside a potato grown in the same field. A man named Ziegland jilted his sweetheart. Her brother tried to avenge his sister's suicide by shooting Ziegland, but the bullet only grazed his face and buried itself in a tree. The brother then ended his own life. Twenty years later Ziegland was blowing up the tree with dynamite. The explosion sent the old bullet through Ziegland's head killing him.

Then there is teleportation which ignores time and space. Probably the most famous historical example was the Spanish soldier who was teleported from the Philippines to Mexico City in the year 1593, but there are other instances not so well known.

Then there is time travel, one of the most popular themes in science-fiction. But is it mere fantasy or does it occasionally happen? As reported in *Mysteries of the Unknown* (Time Life Books), Dr. Edward Moon took a walk one day alone. His constitutional was along an isolated rural road. Coming around a bend the doctor noticed a man approaching him. The stranger was clad in 18th century clothes. Both men stopped and gazed at each other in astonishment. Then the man from out of the past vanished.

A much more detailed contact with the past was once experienced by Mrs. Edna Hedges of Wiltshire, England. One afternoon she was cycling along Ermine Road near Swindon on her way to visit a friend. Heavy dark clouds foretold the approach of a storm. She noticed a thatched cottage at the end of a short lane and decided to ask for shelter. An old man answered the door and beckoned her in.

She remembered that he was grey-bearded, rather tall and was wearing a green waistcoat. He was very friendly and smiled a lot. The rooms were low-ceilinged and dark, but there was a bright fire in the fireplace. After the storm passed she continued her journey. At her friend's house she met some people who had cycled through the storm. They were wet, but her clothing was dry.

Then Mrs. Hedges was told that there was only the dilapidated remains of a structure at the location she gave, unoccupied for at least fifty years. Later, when she returned to the scene, she found only the weed-covered ruins of a foundation.

Whatever the forces are that create these space-time warps, they may have a definite rhythm thus making certain spots freakish and unpredictable. Such a place must be the gardens of the Petit Trianon at Versailles, near Paris, France. Here in August, 1901, Misses Anne Moberly and Eleanor Jourdain, two English teachers from Oxford on a holiday, visited the gardens for an afternoon. They noticed with some surprise that other persons and gardeners were wearing period clothing later determined to be about the time of Marie Antoinette. There is much more about this most famous example of "phantom scenery" and it will be found in a book written by the two ladies entitled *An Adventure After Nine Years of Map and Record Study.*

For our purposes here we note the following facts: This was not a case of mere stored images, an Akashic vision with no consciousness in evidence. They were noticed by persons they met. Twice they asked for and received directions on how to reach the Petit Trianon. Once a youth offered to show them the way to the Cour d'Honneur. A strange feeling of depression and loneliness heralded their journey into the past. Publication of their book brought forth similar accounts of visions by both tourists and nearby residents.

Is it remotely possible that someday in the dusty records of Trianon history will be found an account of how a pair of oddly attired female ghosts came haunting the gardens in broad daylight?

Is it possible that space and time can be stretched or compressed like a piece of chewing gum? Colin Wilson, in his book *Enigmas and Mysteries,* tells of incidents in which motorists have traveled long distances in short periods of time. For example Dr. Arthur Guirdham, an English psychiatrist, and his wife, were astonished one afternoon when they found they had covered twelve miles of country roads in less than five minutes.

It is, however, in occurrences like the following that the mystery of space-time warps reaches heights close to incredible. This account, written by Ken Meaux, appears in *Strange* magazine (Vol. 1, No. 2).

The place was on Highway 167 between Abbeville and Lafayette, Louisiana. The time was October 20, 1969, in the early afternoon on a picture-perfect autumn day. The two businessmen were driving north when they noticed an old turtle-back-type auto moving slowly ahead of them. When they pulled up behind the vehicle they found it to be in mint condition and on the large orange license plate was clearly printed the year 1940.

Passing the antique to the left, they noticed the driver was a young woman wearing a fur coat and a hat bearing a long colored feather. Standing on the seat beside her was a small child wearing a heavy coat and cap. Moreover the windows of the car were rolled up, all very puzzling in view of the mild temperature. Then they observed the expressions of fear and panic on the woman's face. She was looking frantically back and forth as if lost or in need of help. She appeared on the verge of tears.

The man on the passenger's side called out to her and asked if she needed help. She nodded "yes" and as she did so she looked at their modern car with a very puzzled expression. The passenger motioned to her to pull over and park on the side of the road. Again she nodded. They passed her and drove onto the road's shoulder so she could pull up behind them.

When they got out of their car and looked back, they discovered to their astonishment that the antique auto had vanished. There were no side roads where the car could have gone in those brief seconds, no brush or trees to conceal it, just open clear highway. As they stood there in bewilderment, the driver of a car that had been behind the old vehicle pulled over behind them. He jumped out and ran over to the two businessmen excitedly wanting to know what had happened to the car ahead of him. He said he had watched as the old car started to pull up behind the first auto, then in an instant it was gone. It had simply disappeared.

His first thought was that an accident had occurred, but what had happened was perhaps as tragic and far more mysterious. For some time the three men walked around the area discussing the mystery. They gave up the idea of calling the police. No officers on this plane of existence had the power to find the auto and its occupants. They would only question the sanity of the witnesses and test them for intoxication. The men exchanged names, addresses and phone numbers, and for several years they called one another just to discuss the incident and see if any new ideas had developed. None had.

This bizarre occurrence of involuntary time travel raises some interesting questions: Did the woman and child ever return to the world of 1940? If she remained in our time, is she elderly and living somewhere puzzled about her past? Or was this woman and child caught in the web of eternity destined to move in and out of various time zones perhaps forever? We shall never know.

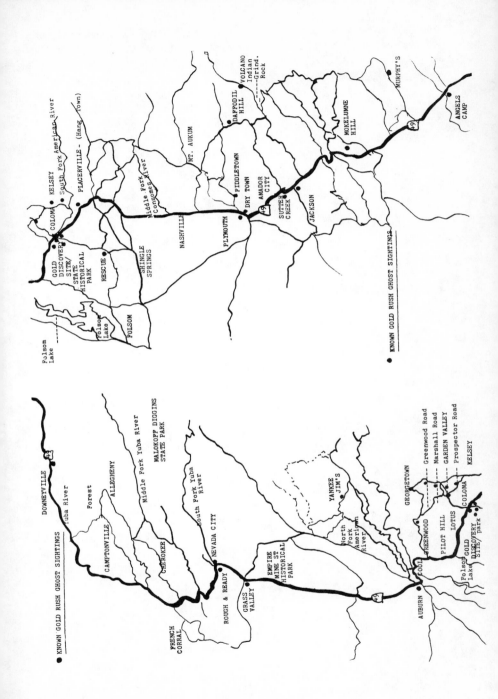

-109-